Positive Behavior Support in Secondary Schools

The Guilford Practical Intervention in the Schools Series

Kenneth W. Merrell, *Founding Editor*
T. Chris Riley-Tillman, *Series Editor*

This series presents the most reader-friendly resources available in key areas of evidence-based practice in school settings. Practitioners will find trustworthy guides on effective behavioral, mental health, and academic interventions, and assessment and measurement approaches. Covering all aspects of planning, implementing, and evaluating high-quality services for students, books in the series are carefully crafted for everyday utility. Features include ready-to-use reproducibles, lay-flat binding to facilitate photocopying, appealing visual elements, and an oversized format.

Positive Behavior Support in Secondary Schools

A Practical Guide

ELLIE L. YOUNG
PAUL CALDARELLA
MICHAEL J. RICHARDSON
K. RICHARD YOUNG

THE GUILFORD PRESS
New York   London

© 2012 The Guilford Press
A Division of Guilford Publications, Inc.
72 Spring Street, New York, NY 10012
www.guilford.com

Printed in the United States of America

This book is printed on acid-free paper.

Last digit is print number: 9   8   7   6   5   4   3   2   1

The authors have checked with sources believed to be reliable in their efforts to provide information that is complete and generally in accord with the standards of practice that are accepted at the time of publication. However, in view of the possibility of human error or changes in behavioral, mental health, or medical sciences, neither the authors, nor the editor and publisher, nor any other party who has been involved in the preparation or publication of this work warrants that the information contained herein is in every respect accurate or complete, and they are not responsible for any errors or omissions or the results obtained from the use of such information. Readers are encouraged to confirm the information contained in this book with other sources.

Library of Congress Cataloging-in-Publication Data

Positive behavior support in secondary schools : a practical guide / Ellie L. Young ... [et al.].
    p. cm. — (The Guilford practical intervention in the schools series)
    Includes bibliographical references and index.
    ISBN 978-1-60918-973-0 (pbk.)
    1. School psychology—United States.   2. Behavior modification—United States.   3. School children—United States—Discipline.   4. High school students—United States—Psychology.
5. Middle school students—United States—Psychology.   I. Young, Ellie L.
    LB1027.55.P67 2012
    373.1102′4—dc23
                                                                                              2011033271

In memory of Kenneth W. Merrell,
who supported our efforts from the beginning
and throughout the writing process

Ken was an encouraging mentor and friend to many of us
over the years. He was a wonderful scholar whose work
made a direct contribution to facilitating positive change
for children and youth.

About the Authors

Ellie L. Young, PhD, NCSP, is Associate Professor at Brigham Young University, in Provo, Utah, where she is coordinator for the School Psychology Graduate Program. Dr. Young practiced as a school psychologist for 9 years in Kansas and Missouri. Her research focuses on screening in secondary settings and gender issues in education. She maintains a small private practice where she works with youth and their families.

Paul Caldarella, PhD, is Director of the Positive Behavior Support Initiative and joint-appointment Associate Professor in the Department of Counseling Psychology and Special Education at Brigham Young University. He served a 1-year internship in child clinical psychology at Arkansas Children's Hospital and a postdoctoral fellowship in adolescent clinical psychology at Bradley Hospital/Brown University. Dr. Caldarella is both a psychologist and certified school psychologist in the state of Utah. His research interests include assessment and intervention for at-risk youth.

Michael J. Richardson, PhD, is Assistant Professor in the Teacher Education Department at Brigham Young University. He has worked with youth, their parents, and teachers in district youth-in-custody programs, in state youth corrections and family services, and as an in-home family preservation consultant for Utah Youth Village. Dr. Richardson's teaching and research centers on adolescent development and student and teacher perceptions of behavior problems in schools.

K. Richard Young, PhD, is Dean of the David O. McKay School of Education and Professor in the Department of Counseling Psychology and Special Education at Brigham Young University. Dr. Young has had experience both as a teacher and as a principal in public schools. He is a licensed psychologist and a former professor at Utah State University, where he also codirected the Institute for the Study of Children, Youth and Families at Risk. Dr. Young has published widely on both academic and social topics in education. The prevention and treatment of emotional and behavioral disorders among at-risk children are the primary foci of his research.

Acknowledgments

This book is the result of many contributions from university colleagues and students, field-based teachers and administrators, and youth who inspire us with their resilience and hope. We are grateful for the thoughtful editing skills of Sharon Black. Other contributors who helped with a variety of tasks that involved literature reviews and manuscript formatting include Ben Young, Ryan Shatzer, and Stacie Gibbons.

Individually, we would like to express additional thanks to others who supported our work.

Ellie: Paul, Mike, and Richard have been patient, thoughtful colleagues. I'm honored to work with them. My parents, Elling and Lou Wright, have believed in me and supported my educational and professional endeavors always. I am most grateful. My husband and children, Frank, Erin, Frank-o, and Erik, have been more than patient with my time spent writing and attending meetings. Their laughter, joy, and prayers mean everything to me.

Paul: I am grateful for my loving parents, who first instilled in me a desire to help others. Thank you to my dear wife, Andrea, who has been a continued source of resilience and fortitude despite the many changes we have made in our lives. I am grateful for my children, AJ and Andrew, for providing daily respite from the world of work and from whom I learn every day. Finally, thank you to my coauthors: Ellie L. Young, for keeping this project on track and moving forward; Michael J. Richardson, for his willingness to diligently and competently do whatever was needed; and, finally, K. Richard Young, who first hired me as a graduate student over 15 years ago and has continued to support my professional development ever since.

Mike: I would like to thank my wife, Allison, for never letting me give up; my parents, Ed and Kathleen, for showing me how to instill a love of learning in an adolescent student; and my children, for their enthusiasm, which is better than medicine. I would also like to thank my fellow authors for inviting my participation in this project and for their friendship in spite of it.

Richard: I am grateful to my doctoral chair, colleague, and dear friend Howard Sloane, who passed away in 2010. Howard was a great mentor and teacher; he started me on a career that I have always enjoyed. I appreciate the many children, with special needs and risks, who have taught me much in regard to educating children and youth. Likewise, I have learned much from my own children, and I love and respect each of them for all they have accomplished in their lives. I express my indebtedness to loving parents who nurtured and taught me throughout their lives. Thanks to my greatest and most patient teacher, my wife of more than 40 years, Janet. And thanks to three great colleagues: Ellie, Paul, and Michael.

This book is based, in part, on research funded by an Office of Special Education Programs (OESP) Federal Grant (H324c030124).

Preface

This book is a guide for secondary school–based teams that are planning to implement or are in the process of implementing a schoolwide positive behavior support (SWPBS) model. As youth enter and move through adolescence, their needs for behavioral and emotional support are distinct from those of elementary school students. These students need autonomy, strong social networks, cognitive challenges, and academic growth. Adolescent students also face considerable risks and challenges that may not have been evident during their childhood years. During this time, they are at greater risk for mental health disorders and they are more likely to exhibit symptoms of anxiety, depression, or antisocial behaviors. Bullying and victimization are more likely to occur in junior high and middle school settings. Academic demands increase as students enter secondary schools, with expectations for independent work and organizational skills continuing to expand through high school until graduation.

Addressing the behavioral and emotional needs of youth in secondary schools is often challenging because of the emphasis on preparing students to succeed in postsecondary settings and in high-stakes testing. Research has long supported that meeting the emotional and behavioral needs of students has a positive influence on academic achievement. Implementing an SWPBS model is an effective way of meeting the needs of secondary students. The process of implementing an SWPBS model essentially involves screening, providing responsive interventions, and measuring progress. Even though the model is straightforward, implementing it in secondary settings requires awareness and responsiveness to the structure and organization of these settings. This book fine-tunes and adapts the implementation process to the specific needs of secondary students and the educators who care about them.

Readers are encouraged to review the table of contents, reflect on their level of current implementation of SWPBS, and determine where to start reading. The book was designed as a start-to-finish implementation guide, but it is possible to begin with chapters that best match the needs of the school team's current level of implementation. However, understanding the fundamental or theoretical principles that support a sustainable SWPBS is imperative. Although this book can be a great help to team leaders, all members of the SWPBS team are encouraged to read and become familiar with the concepts in the chapters in order to plan and evaluate activities.

Chapter 1 begins with an explanation of the guiding principles of behavior and how behaviors can be changed. We include a discussion of the role of the environment in facilitating behavioral change. A teaching approach to discipline is compared to a coercive, reactive response to unacceptable behavior. Key components of SWPBS and a three-tiered approach are described.

The developmental changes of adolescence (physical, cognitive, and social) are addressed in Chapter 2. Autonomy, identity, self-concepts, and moral awareness are discussed, and the strengths and challenges of meeting these needs in secondary settings are explored.

Chapter 3 focuses on school climate and why it is important. The benefits and components of a healthy school climate are presented. Ways of measuring school climate and maintaining a sustained focus on preventing problem behaviors are key parts of this chapter.

Planning for schoolwide implementation by assembling a team, identifying resources, and creating buy-in from teachers and other stakeholders are the principal ideas in Chapter 4. Major points of this chapter involve working with parents, students, and district administrators. Important ideas for designing teacher development are included.

Chapters 5 and 6 focus on the actual implementation and monitoring of schoolwide, or Tier 1, interventions. Explicit instruction of behaviors and social skills is discussed in depth, as is the use of praise and token economies as ways of reinforcing learning and appropriate behaviors. Using data to determine needs and establishing a system for making data-based decisions are stressed. The strengths and weaknesses of frequently using office discipline referrals to monitor outcomes are presented.

The necessity of screening to identify students whose needs are not met through schoolwide support is discussed in Chapter 7. Characteristics of effective screening instruments, approvals needed for screening, and examples of screening measures are provided.

Interventions for Tiers 2 and 3 are discussed in Chapters 8 and 9, respectively. Focusing on small-group interventions, Chapter 8 presents specific ideas that could be used to meet the needs of secondary students. Chapter 9 focuses on many of the same interventions discussed in Chapter 8 but adapts the principles for individualized interventions.

Chapter 10 defines sustainability and integrates ideas presented throughout the book to help the reader plan for sustainability from the beginning of the implementation process. We encourage readers to understand and work toward sustainability even before beginning this process.

Contents

10. Sustainability and Maintenance   137

References   145

Index   153

List of Figures, Tables, and Forms

FIGURES

TABLES

FORMS

CHAPTER 1

Foundational Ideas

Educators today face challenges on a number of fronts. The principal of a high school of over 900 students reported that as many as 50 students per week were referred to his office for behavior problems. Another principal was frustrated because 39 different languages were spoken in her school, and many students did not speak English well enough to read basic texts or write well enough to complete simple assignments. A high school teacher was teaching 206 different students in six academic periods each day, including 23 students with disabilities and 37 others who were at serious risk for school failure. Educators must confront increasing discipline problems, student apathy or lack of engagement, school violence, various types of bullying (e.g., cyberbullying, relational aggression), poor literacy skills, increasing numbers of students leaving school before graduation, problems with absenteeism and tardies, and innumerable additional challenges. (We define educators as individuals employed in a school who contribute to learning outcomes, including, but not limited to, general education teachers, special education teachers, school psychologists, school counselors, administrators, para-educators, social workers, speech pathologists, and behavioral specialists.)

Underlying many of these difficulties and exacerbating others is the fading of civility from our schools and communities (Hinckley, 2000), a concern of educators and community members as well. Civility includes positive behaviors of courtesy, respect, and kindness that are needed to help students be successful in school, society, democratic government, and employment. To intensify these challenges state and federal governments are increasing expectations and accountability.

This plethora of problems contributes to weak student outcomes in both academic and social–emotional areas. As students misbehave, tune out, withdraw, or turn their anger toward others, they miss opportunities to develop and display needed competencies. In addition to weakness in academic areas, schools may not be facilitating healthy social–emotional learning and behaviors. The purpose of this book is to share with fellow educators ideas and strategies that have been effective in a comprehensive schoolwide system to support youth in gaining and maintaining needed behavioral, social–emotional, and relational skills in secondary schools.

1

GUIDING PRINCIPLES

Underlying the design and implementation of sustainable, theory-driven interventions for youth who have or who are at risk for emotional and behavioral problems are basic assumptions or guiding principles that make such prevention strategies and interventions responsive to the needs of students and community. Understanding the concepts and premises of a comprehensive approach to prevention and intervention is critical to developing programs that improve student outcomes.

Needs and Behavior

The first principle of intervention is that all youth can learn to meet their needs through their appropriate behavior. Learning begins at birth and continues throughout life. Sometimes learned behavior is negative or problematic, even if it meets one's needs. All behavior has a purpose and communicates need. For example, a crying infant may communicate hunger, thirst, or discomfort, and parents respond by identifying and meeting that need. The child learns to cry to get his or her needs met. This pattern continues through childhood and extends into adolescence; in fact, it continues through life. Similarly, an adolescent may learn that physical fighting is a way of solving conflict with peers or establishing oneself as a peer group leader. Students learn to communicate that they lack academic skills or that they find the assignment boring by refusing to complete school assignments. Problematic behavior is rarely taught intentionally, but it is learned incidentally as a natural consequence of everyday behavior. Parents and teachers certainly don't want children to learn to fight, refuse to follow directions, or engage in other negative behavior. If a negative behavior like fighting serves a purpose, intervention might include ways to achieve the same results without the negative consequences. As adults our goal is to teach children and youth to meet real needs with socially competent behavior.

> **All behavior has a purpose and communicates need.**

This goal can best be achieved when educators focus more of their time and efforts on building positive skills and dispositions rather than waiting for problem behaviors to appear and then concentrate on eliminating problems. A familiar analogy represents two choices: Do you build a sturdy fence at the top of the cliff to prevent people from falling off, or do you provide an ambulance at the bottom to pick up the victims? Educators will be effective if they focus on building strong, attractive, positive fences that can withstand challenges and tests in addition to knowing how to respond to unanticipated problems. These fences can be adapted as needs change.

> **Problematic behavior is rarely taught intentionally, but it is learned incidentally as a natural consequence of everyday behavior.**

Replacements for Problem Behavior

One of the most important guiding principles of our work as educators is to *replace problem behavior with positive behavior and provide meaningful reinforcement.* For example, a student who fights to resolve peer conflict could be taught strategies for understanding and addressing conflict in ways that do not involve potential injury or punitive school discipline. He or she can become more aware of his or her emotions and of the point when he or she might lose control; he or she can learn to avoid situations that are likely to result in conflict; he or she can learn a problem-solving strategy by which he or she considers the consequences of his or her actions; or he can learn to discuss conflicts, either with an adult mentor or peer group.

> **Replace problem behavior with positive behavior and provide meaningful reinforcement.**

When the student begins learning and using these new behaviors, he or she will be reinforced through improved relationships with peers and adults and through improved academic outcomes. He or she will also have more learning time because he or she is no longer missing school due to suspensions or addressing other disciplinary issues. Focusing on helping students to learn and use replacement behaviors facilitates a teaching approach to discipline, which will be discussed later in the chapter.

Beliefs That Facilitate Change

Educators should also consider the following principles in designing and implementing interventions that address the behavioral, social, and emotional needs of students.

- All youth can develop prosocial behavior associated with school and lifelong success if they have sufficient opportunities to be taught the new skills and practice them.
- Educators must use evidence-based practices that are tailored to the specific needs of students in the contexts of classrooms, schools, and general life situations if they are to facilitate meaningful positive change.
- Sufficient practice with timely, constructive feedback must be provided to ensure mastery of social skills and internalization of civil, respectful behavior.
- All school personnel, parents, siblings, peers, and community members can share in responsibility for the intervention through positive and gentle corrective feedback, which includes caring words and actions that express encouragement.
- Learning occurs most readily when teachers and parents have developed and maintain relationships of trust and mutual respect. The learning environment should feel safe, secure, and hopeful rather than threatening and coercive.
- Adults should adopt high but reasonable expectations for both academic learning and civil behavior, along with low tolerance (but not zero tolerance) for unacceptable behavior. This approach does not require threats and punishment if it focuses on teaching new skills and strategies and also provides positive feedback, encouragement, and praise. Instruction must focus on building skills rather than just eliminating undesirable behavior.
- A teaching approach to skill building often requires patiently repeating the instructions over time while providing corrective feedback and enthusiastically recognizing progress.

A TEACHING APPROACH TO DISCIPLINE

Discipline is critical in establishing a safe and positive school with an environment conducive to learning. A teaching approach to discipline has enduring results because new behaviors are taught and learned. Teaching acceptable behavior requires us to remember that behavior is functional, predictable, and changeable (Crone & Horner, 2003). We begin with a discussion of general principles of teaching acceptable behaviors.

Teaching Acceptable Behaviors

> Environments can be punishing or reinforcing, consistent or unpredictable. The way in which educators combine these elements can make teaching more or less effective. We can design and create environments that target and teach positive behaviors.

The consequences of a particular behavior shape and influence future displays of that behavior. Environments can be punishing or reinforcing, consistent or unpredictable. The way in which educators combine these elements can make teaching more or less effective. We can design and create environments that target and teach positive behaviors.

Previous outcomes and consequences of behavior teach which behaviors work and which behaviors are unlikely to get the desired results. Behavior becomes automatic once it is learned, repeated, and reinforced sufficiently. Behavior changes as individuals learn alternative ways to respond to events. When new behaviors lead to outcomes that are more useful or desirable than previous ineffective behaviors, the new positive behavior tends to be repeated. For example, if teachers consistently call on only students who raise their hand to speak in class, most youth quickly learn to raise their hands rather than shouting out answers.

When students exhibit such civil and cooperative behaviors and teachers reinforce such behaviors, teachers and students develop warm and trusting relationships. In turn, an instructional environment that is effective for the whole class develops. Conversely, a few experiences may teach a student that tripping other students in the hall is not the most effective or socially acceptable strategy for gaining attention, or that bullying, which may have had desired outcomes in the past, may lead to a punishing visit with a school administrator or a painful apology to the other student. Through teaching interactions, a student may learn that polite language, spoken in a calm voice, is more effective for expressing concerns than swearing at an authority figure or a peer.

Side Effects of Coercion

When students misbehave we can assume that their behavior has a function that falls into one of several broad categories: getting attention from someone, avoiding or escaping painful or uncomfortable circumstances, or obtaining something the individual wants (Sidman, 1989). For example, a teen may fight with a peer to get the peer's attention or to help the aggressor obtain a sense of power and an opportunity to manipulate the peer.

When youth display aggressive, troubling, or noncompliant behavior, adults frequently use punishment and threats of punishment to stop the misbehavior, which Sidman (1989) defines as *coercion*. Coercive methods of behavior management have limited effectiveness: They may be reinforcing for adults because they suppress a particular behavior quickly, but they rarely change a student's behavior permanently. Punishment that is harsh enough to create lasting change tends to have unintended negative consequences that damage relationships. When adults use coercion, some side effects that can be observed with students include escape, avoidance, resentment, disrespect, and aggression. The student may turn to countercoercion by inflicting pain on others; the student avoids or escapes the person who punished him or her. Serious types of escape and avoidance behaviors include the use of drugs and alcohol, school absenteeism, withdrawal from others, and drop out from school or society at large (Sidman). Perhaps the most toxic side effect is avoiding the people associated with the aversive situation, such as teachers and parents, who have the potential to teach new behaviors and build meaningful relationships. Thus by avoiding the punisher the youth may also avoid needed sources of help and support.

> Coercive methods of behavior management have limited effectiveness: They may be reinforcing for adults because they suppress a particular behavior quickly, but they rarely change a student's behavior permanently.

Threats and punishment by adults tend to be quick emotional responses caused by the understandable frustration. They may seem justified, but they are ultimately not effective. Table 1.1 provides a comparison of two contrasting approaches to discipline: coercion and instruction (adapted from Black & Downs, 1987). Discipline is most effective when a student is taught behavior that is both socially acceptable and efficient in meeting his or her needs. Mild forms of punishment such as time out, exclusion, or extra practice at times that are inconvenient to the student are effective with minimal side effects when combined with teaching and positive reinforcements for appropriate behavior.

TABLE 1.1. A Comparison of Two Approaches to Discipline

	Coercion: Using threats and punishment to eliminate problem behavior	Instruction: Teaching alternative positive behavior
Why is the approach typically used?	To stop the behavior annoying the adult by issuing penalties, making threats, or inflicting pain (physical, mental, or emotional).	To correct problems by teaching appropriate skills that help the child develop maturity, civility, and self-discipline.
What is the focus of the teachers or parents?	The past or immediate problem behavior—a short-term perspective.	Skills for success in school and life—a long-term perspective.
What is the emotional context in which the method is used?	The adult is often angry, hostile, frustrated, physically tense, and stressed.	The adult is calm and relaxed, with feelings of care and concern for the individual's success and well-being.
What are the potential results or side effects experienced by the student?	Thoughts or feelings of fear, guilt, stupidity, inferiority, lack of confidence, anger, hostility, and contempt.	Thoughts or feelings of confidence, value, self-worth, and trust in others, with a desire to reciprocate the acts of kindness, care, and concern.

Creating a Supportive Environment

The environment in which the learning takes place is an important variable that greatly impacts outcomes. Learning occurs best in environments that are positive, warm, safe, and predictable. Without such an environment, the learner may be so preoccupied with unrelated issues that little learning occurs. For example, a student may be worried about walking home from school through an area where gangs are prominent; or a student who needs help in understanding an academic concept may be afraid to ask his or her teacher for fear of ridicule. Most teachers have seen a student standing alone in a crowded area, afraid to approach others after past rejection.

Teacher Behavior

The teacher is central to any learning environment. Teachers who model acts of kindness and demonstrate civility create positive environments for learning. Teachers who invite and answer questions or respond politely with patience and understanding when asked for help create a context for learning that is safe and secure. Students feel comfortable with taking risks such as asking and answering questions, sharing responses, and generating and expressing critical new ideas. These teachers encourage learning. All teachers can exemplify acting with civility, speaking politely, and engaging in socially appropriate behavior. Teachers who exhibit harsh, critical, or threatening behaviors typically inhibit learning.

High Expectations

Positive, civil behavior needs to be accompanied by high expectations for both academic learning and social conduct. Acting in a kind, caring manner does not mean accepting rude, aggressive, vulgar, or otherwise inappropriate behavior from students. Neither children nor adults grow and thrive in environments with low expectations or acceptance of socially unacceptable, hurtful actions. Expectations need to be taught, encouraged, and positively reinforced. Expectations must be clear and specific. They need to challenge the learners at appropriate levels, levels that require reaching and stretching. Negative responses such as reprimands, harsh words, and criticism usually do not inspire learners to try again or to persist until they achieve mastery. When students and teachers view mistakes as opportunities to learn rather than errors to be punished, students are more likely to feel motivated and supported. Repeated learning opportunities help in mastery of new skills and ensure that new knowledge is accurate. Learners need to receive correct information and then have opportunities for active, engaged participation. The best learning environments promote engagement and interaction among all learners and provide corrective feedback in a supportive manner. In such contexts students and educators learn from each other.

> **When students and teachers view mistakes as opportunities to learn rather than errors to be punished, students are more likely to feel motivated and supported.**

Beginning Strategies

If you are establishing a learning environment or observing one in order to provide support for teachers and students, you may want to consider the following activities:

1. Make a list of a few key positive behaviors that can be both taught and modeled for students. Monitor your behavior to be sure that you are an example of the behavior you want to teach.

2. Establish an environment that is reinforcing for students, an environment where (a) they succeed with academic assignments; (b) they receive positive feedback regularly; (c) they experience positive social interactions with classmates and adults; (d) they engage in learning activities that are challenging, exciting, and interesting; and (e) they look forward to coming to class each day.

3. Establish a few rules or expectations that state positive, expected behaviors. Post the rules where they can be easily seen and serve as a reminder. Teach the expectations to the students using examples of behaviors that comply with the rules, but also provide nonexamples so students can see and identify behaviors that do not comply. This contrast helps students discriminate clearly. Have students develop both examples and nonexamples of their own. Also clearly teach the consequences for following and not following the rules. Teach the expectations frequently, rather than just at the beginning of the school year. When problems arise, reteach. This topic will be discussed in more depth in Chapter 5.

4. Directly teach the social skills that assist students in getting along with peers and adults. Social skills such as speaking politely, interacting respectfully, following requests from adults in charge, complimenting others, receiving compliments graciously, inviting others to participate in activities, asking politely for help, and showing appreciation go a long way in helping all students achieve success in school. (Chapter 5 has more in-depth information about teaching social skills.) Teach all students basic routines that help the classroom and school function efficiently. Some examples include (a) how to transition between activities, (b) how to be inclusive in both social and academic activities, (c) how to behave respectively when someone is performing or speaking to a group, and (d) how to eat in the school cafeteria or in other public and private places with good manners and dignity.

Teaching such behaviors at the beginning of a school year makes them part of the classroom and school routine, saving much time for academic activities. These behaviors must be taught with respect and patience, with positive examples and opportunities for positive practices in a favorable teaching environment.

POSITIVE BEHAVIOR SUPPORT

Positive behavior support is a model that was developed from research conducted in the fields of applied behavior analysis, special education, and school psychology. Focused on eliminating behavior problems with positive strategies instead of punishment, this research progressed toward development of positive interventions based in environmental support systems. The goal of providing support for individuals developed further into a conceptual framework designed to serve all students in a school.

The purpose of schoolwide positive behavior support (SWPBS) is to create school environments that focus on preventing and reducing problem behavior while promoting and supporting academic achievement and prosocial development for all students (Turnbull et al., 2002). SWPBS and response to intervention (RTI) share many core features. SWPBS and RTI emphasize the use of data for making decisions about student and system needs. Both models also conceptualize interventions systems as tiers, a concept discussed in the next section. Both RTI and SWPBS focus on developing a continuum of services and interventions that are systematically developed based on students' measured skill levels. Similarly, both consider the environment's role when problems occur (Sandomierski, Kincaid, & Algozzine, 2007). SWPBS programs are carried out by school personnel with the support of teams that provide leadership and technical assistance. Historically, RTI research has focused on early identification and intervention for academic problems. Having a strong core curriculum with evidence-based instruction so that academic problems are prevented from the onset is another foundation component of RTI. The main difference between SWPBS and RTI is that the former tends to focus on student behavior and emotional needs and the latter focuses on academic needs, but essentially the processes integrated into the models are quite similar.

> **The purpose of SWPBS is to create school environments that focus on preventing and reducing problem behavior while promoting and supporting academic achievement and prosocial development for all students.**

Key Components of SWPBS

SWPBS is not a set of prescribed procedures that must be used the same way in all schools (Renshaw, Young, Caldarella, & Christensen, 2008). Rather, it is a systems approach structured by a set of three flexible and adaptable guiding elements (Sugai & Horner, 2006), and the three-tiered continuum of student support (Turnbull et al., 2002). The three-tiered continuum is depicted in Figure 1.1.

The guiding elements are four foundational, interactive processes that are to be carried out when initially establishing or recalibrating SWPBS. Grounded in behavioral science, these processes are the backbone of the practice because they (1) establish measurable and achievable long-term outcomes; (2) identify empirically supported practices to achieve those outcomes; (3) use data to make decisions, identify needs, and monitor student progress toward specific outcomes; and (4) establish formal system supports (e.g., personnel, funding, and training) to increase sustainability (Sugai & Horner, 2006). Given that these processes can be accomplished through various practices and procedural combinations, we would expect SWPBS to look somewhat different from school to school. But despite this expected variance, at least one feature of SWPBS rarely varies: the schema for conceptualizing student's needs—a tiered continuum of student support that is responsive to student needs (Renshaw et al., 2008) and facilitates a comprehensive approach.

A Three-Tiered Approach

A well-known approach to developing a continuum of services is represented in Figure 1.1 with three tiers of preventions or interventions that can be adapted to meet the needs of all students. Each tier focuses on outcomes and data. Team meetings are not spent admiring the problem,

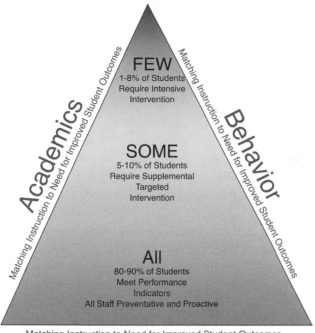

FIGURE 1.1. The triangle of continuum of services. From Utah Professional Development Center *wiki.updc.org/abc*. Reprinted with permission.

describing it in vague terms, or offering simple solutions such as just encouraging the student to try harder. School teams that are developing a continuum of services can evaluate current programs and decide whether data support the continued use of specific programs. Existing worthwhile programs may be modified into a continuum of services to meet varied student needs. For example, some schools may have after-school academic tutoring with specific teachers, tracking systems for academic assignments, and social skills groups led by school psychologists or school counselors. Increasing collaboration among those leading these interventions can begin to merge services into a continuum so that students who have a combination of academic and social problems can receive coordinated services.

Having separate or uncoordinated programs tends to foster an isolationist environment in schools. A program may be perceived as serving a narrow group of students: for example, tutoring programs are only for students with difficulties in literacy, not for those with behavioral problems, anxiety disorders, or math problems who may need just a bit more help in these areas. When educators communicate an attitude of "That's not my problem" or a mindset of "That's not my job," solitary programming is probably the result. In contrast, with a continuum of services the data are used to determine what *interventions* (rather than programs) are relevant to and needed for current

> **With a continuum of services the data are used to determine what *interventions* (rather than programs) are relevant to and needed for current problems. The focus is on student outcomes, data, interventions, and problem solving rather than developing and maintaining programs.**

problems. The focus is on student outcomes, data, interventions, and problem solving rather than developing and maintaining programs.

A comprehensive approach provides a continuum of services so that students have access to interventions that are responsive to their levels of needs. For example, a new seventh grader who hides in the bathroom during class breaks because he or she is intimidated by noisy crowds needs a different type of support than a student who is sent to the office at least once a day for yelling at teachers and swearing in class. Some students may be fighting in the hall frequently, while others quietly struggle with finding someone to sit with during lunch. The variety of these student concerns demonstrates a range of needs. In a comprehensive system each student is able to learn new behaviors tailored to his or her situation. The school personnel and the support team must understand the variety of student needs in order to develop interventions to meet those needs.

Some schools develop isolated programs for which students must qualify in order to participate. Students who do not qualify do not have their needs met. Some schools have an assortment of programs for students, but the programs may not be coordinated or may not reflect the range of student needs. When a continuum of services is provided, administrators are not likely to say "We don't have a program for that," because varied interventions have been flexibly designed to meet student needs.

For example, Tyler's eighth-grade English teacher noticed that he was sleeping in class and irritating peers when he was awake. The teacher sometimes heard Tyler threatening to fight another student at lunch. He was not turning in assignments and was barely earning a C in the class. Other teachers reported similar concerns. The assistant principal reported that Tyler had been sent to the office six times during the past month for noncompliant and disorderly conduct in several classes. Rather than waiting for Tyler to fail English (and probably other classes) and spend more time in the office, the SWPBS support team developed a self-monitoring program to help Tyler and his parents know when assignments would be due. Tyler was taught the social skill of following directions, and teachers were asked to meaningfully reinforce this specific behavior. Within 2 weeks, Tyler's grades showed improvement, and his referrals to the office had decreased. He was still spending some time in the office for noncompliant behavior, and he continued to experience some conflicts in his peer relationships, but progress was monitored by tracking grades and office disciplinary referrals (ODRs). Tyler's problems were addressed through an integrated intervention focused on teaching new behaviors before problems became overwhelming. Tyler's problems were dealt with before they became so substantial that many resources would be needed. The team avoided the "wait-to-fail" approach: Tyler got what he needed when he needed it.

When services are adapted to individual students, small problems can be solved before they become bigger problems. As the magnitude of the problems decrease, less intrusive or intense services are made available. Using a three-tiered approach to addressing student needs helps match services to students' needs.

Tier 1

Tier 1 (the bottom of the triangle) also has been termed *primary prevention* or the *universal* tier. Efforts at this tier provide highly effective, core curricular strategies that meet the needs of the general school population and focus on preventing problems before they occur. Tier 1 efforts work toward making the school an effective, proactive, caring environment. Strategies might include having research-supported curricula so that academic problems are less likely to happen. Ensuring that the core curricula and instruction are engaging and relevant can be important in preventing behavior problems. Creating positive, clear, and specific behavioral expectations for the whole school is another crucial facet of the Tier 1 platform. Suicide prevention and schoolwide social skill instruction are other examples of Tier 1 strategies. Any approach that is directed at all students is a Tier 1 tactic—these strategies usually focus on the whole school and the needs of the general student body. However, Tier 1 strategies could just focus on the needs of ninth graders in a junior high school setting if the interventions were only needed by that cohort of students. At this tier there are no selection criteria or eligibility requirements. Efforts are ongoing and focus on strengthening the core curricula that includes behavior and academics. Effective approaches also intervene with individual students as quickly as problems arise. Many problems can be addressed with quick, effective interventions.

Tier 1 activities should be designed to support all students in achieving behavioral and academic success. Teachers frequently collaborate to solve problems promptly. Some consider plans at this level to be prevention rather than intervention because teams anticipate and address problems in a timely manner. Schoolwide data are used to design universal plans. For instance, when reviewing all of the ODRs the team may realize that many of the problems are occurring in the halls before, during, and after lunch. The team might decide to assign three more teachers to provide supervision during this time and reteach behavioral expectations. Additional supervisors could be asked to continually circulate in the lunchroom and adjoining hallways and to review positive behavioral expectations in the lunchroom each week. Teachers and supervisors would consistently praise students who were meeting the behavioral expectations, and they would deal with small infractions quickly. If the team reviewed the data a month later and found that ODRs had decreased 30%, they would probably determine that this supervision should be maintained. Several fights were prevented that would have led to out-of-school suspensions, and administrators spent less time responding to behavior problems and more time providing supervision and instructional leadership. Chapter 5 specifically explores Tier 1 strategies.

Tier 2

Usually about 5–10% of students will not be responsive to universal approaches and will need additional support beyond the core curriculum and what individual teachers or teams usually provide. A process for screening all students is part of the tiered approach; deciding which students need interventions and determining types and timing of those interventions are discussed in Chapters 7, 8, and 9. Tier 2 practices focus on those students whose needs are not met by the universal strategies of Tier 1 and addresses problems that were not solved by Tier 1 approaches. Students who have been identified for Tier 2 participate in Tier 1 activities with the rest of the student body, but also receive additional instruction or support that focuses on their specific problems. Students with similar needs, concerns, and problems are often grouped to facilitate more practice or instruction in problem areas.

The intensity, frequency, and duration of Tier 2 approaches depend on the needs of the students and the data that represent their progress. Students may participate in Tier 2 activities for several weeks or months depending on their measured progress. Examples of Tier 2 interventions, which include attending a social skills group, participating in a self-monitoring program, or joining an after-school tutoring program, are described in Chapter 8.

Tier 3

Tier 3 interventions are the most intensive interventions, tend to last longer than Tier 2 interventions, and focus primarily on individual needs and interventions. Tier 3 is appropriate for those students who do not respond to Tier 2 strategies—typically about 1–8% of the student population. Students receiving this level of support tend to have chronic, complex, long-term problems. Some assessments and interventions at this level include functional assessment of behaviors, individual tracking of behaviors and academics, specific behavioral contracting, and teaching positive replacement behaviors. Chapter 9 focuses on these topics.

Developing a tiered approach that provides a continuum of services is not a simple, straightforward task. Ongoing team effort is required to plan and coordinate services. Teachers or other service providers implementing primarily Tier 1 strategies cannot work in isolation. All stakeholders need to know what is happening across the tiers so that as students move through the tiers students' needs are met. Changes are made as data indicate, and interventions at each tier are developed and implemented effectively and efficiently.

Collaboration across the tiers is essential. Using the example of high numbers of ODRs in the halls during the lunch hour, if ODR data indicate that lunchtime is problematic because students are likely to sneak off campus, get in fights, or be tardy to their next class, responses across the tiers are needed. A Tier 1 approach to this scenario would be to clarify positive behavioral expectations at lunch, increase supervision, and praise students for meeting expectations. The team also may consider providing a schoolwide incentive for improvement (e.g., extra tickets for the school carnival for students when the data indicate that ODRs or tardies are decreasing). A Tier 2 strategy would be appropriate if the data indicated that 50% of the ODRs at lunchtime were given to 5–10 students who were frequently getting in fights. A small-group 6-week intervention focusing on problem solving or anger management could address the problem. If the small-group strategy decreased the ODRs for all but one or two of the students, Tier 3 activities might require gathering additional data for those students who did not respond to Tier 2 strategies.

Tier 3 approaches could include assessing the function of a student's behaviors, conducting individual interviews, and consulting with parents. Depending on the outcome of additional data gathering, individual interventions could be implemented and monitored. If needed, additional community resources can be gathered to contribute to the problem-solving process. To work efficiently, the tiered approach needs to be a coordinated effort rather than isolated, fragmented approaches treating scattered aspects of complex problems.

> **To work efficiently, the tiered approach needs to be a coordinated effort rather than isolated, fragmented approaches treating scattered aspects of complex problems.**

SUMMARY

The challenges facing educators today can be overwhelming and frustrating. Fortunately, research has supported the use of positive strategies to address these formidable problems. Understanding how behaviors are learned and how they can be altered is the basis for creating system change; using and responding to data to develop an integrated approach for creating a continuum of services is fundamental to creating sustainable system change. The following chapters describe what is needed to develop this continuum of services and how teams can work to create an environment that is responsive to *all* student needs.

CHAPTER 2

Adolescent Needs
and Secondary Settings

Mike is a seventh-grade student, new to his junior high. He feels a mixture of excitement and anxiety as he adjusts to being one of the younger students in a "big kid" context instead of being one of the older students in a "little kid" context. On the first day he gets a bit lost finding his classes and is somewhat embarrassed to have to ask for help—revealing his lack of experience and potentially exposing him as a "little kid." But his excitement about having so many new and exciting choices and responsibilities momentarily overrides his embarrassment. In his math class, however, his teacher begins the period by sternly announcing that she dislikes "children," crowding around her desk asking questions. Intimidated, and wanting to avoid any further embarrassment, Mike resolves not to ask any questions at all. He receives his first failing grade in math and begins to develop the belief that he is not good at—and thus not interested in—math.

As students move through secondary schools, developmental challenges both fascinate and frustrate adults and youth. Adolescents experience rapid physical, intellectual, and social changes at different rates and different times, as educational contexts and social expectations may be changing dramatically as well. Although sometimes out of sync with peers, some adolescents might experience physical growth spurts that rival their rate of growth as toddlers. And students' understanding of what is happening around them may be complicated by their own cognitive and emotional development. Developmental and environmental demands contribute to a complex challenge for educators to meet the needs of students while providing meaningful and positive educational experiences.

> **Developmental and environmental demands contribute to a complex challenge for educators to meet the needs of students while providing meaningful and positive educational experiences.**

As many teachers know, challenges often create unique opportunities. Contrary to some popular notions, adolescence can represent a window of opportunity on many fronts. In addition to experiencing rapid intellectual growth, students at this age may also be ready to develop richer and more egalitarian relationships, an enhanced sense of morality, and a positive identity. However, much of this growth depends on the cultivation of environments and relationships that nurture the development of these attributes.

DEVELOPMENTAL CHANGES

In this section we describe some of the changes associated with physical, cognitive, and social development during adolescence in the context of secondary schools. We also suggest some possibilities for how educators might respond to these changes in order to support positive developmental experiences.

Physical

Rapid physical changes during adolescence can pro-duce awkwardness on the one hand and increased confidence on the other—or both—depending in part on timing; gender; preparation from parents, teachers, and peers; and social environments. Adolescents who develop early can sometimes get more attention from

> **Adolescents who develop early can sometimes get more attention from peers, but they also can be at a greater risk of unhealthy behaviors such as substance abuse and sexual promiscuity.**

peers, but they also can be at a greater risk of unhealthy behaviors such as substance abuse and sexual promiscuity. Early-maturing girls may experience a decline in self-image, especially if they experience a shift to secondary education contexts at the same time, whereas early-maturing boys may experience increases in feelings of hostility or distress. Late developers might receive less attention from peers, but they may also develop a stronger orientation toward academic and career goals (Susman & Rogol, 2004).

In addition to the outward changes, adolescents change physically in ways that are less obvious, but that can affect behavior profoundly. Pubertal hormones increase, of course, but the actual levels of hormones may have less impact on emotion than the psychological and environ-mental factors. Many adolescents effectively adapt to these changes, and adults may have even higher (though more stable) levels of the same hormones typically blamed for adolescent mis-behavior (Dahl & Hariri, 2005). However, these hormonal and accompanying physical changes might be experienced as stressful for adolescents in part because of their novelty (Susman & Rogol, 2004). The potential for increased stress during physical development suggests that ado-lescents might need extra emotional support during this time. Educators can be an important source of emotional support by providing ample encouragement and praise regarding positive social, behavioral, and academic efforts—potentially ameliorating the effects of an all too com-mon overemphasis on physical appearance and development. Addressing social conflicts and behavioral challenges can also help establish safe environments where social anxiety and nega-tive peer influences are reduced.

Cognitive

The adolescent brain continues to develop rapidly throughout adolescence. Specifically, con-tinued myelination and synaptic pruning in the prefrontal cortex are thought to contribute to more efficient and perhaps advanced cognitive functioning (Keating, 2004). The pruning of synapses may increase the efficiency of brain function, enabling development of advanced cognitive skills, but it may also reduce specific capabilities for some types of learning (e.g., learning a new language) as synaptic connections that are used less often are eventually pruned.

Although the connection between brain development and cognition is still being explored, it seems clear that adolescents experience increases in deductive reasoning, conscious control in decision making, information-processing efficiency, working memory, and problem solving (Keating, 2004). These changes depend in part on physical maturation; however, effective educational environments are also important for cognitive development. Adolescents need ample opportunities and encouragement to think critically and creatively, of course, which will facilitate academic success. However, educators may sometimes forget that these same developing capacities may allow adolescents to more effectively challenge rules and expectations. Students might more frequently demand rationales both for why they need to learn something and for why they are expected to behave in certain ways. Developing cognitive capacities during adolescence may require educators to more carefully consider and clearly communicate the rationales behind school rules and expectations.

> Adolescents experience increases in deductive reasoning, conscious control in decision making, information-processing efficiency, working memory, and problem solving.

Social

> Secondary education students are in the process of changing social roles, from children to adolescents, and ultimately of being defined by society, and by themselves, as young adults.

Many influences can contribute to or pose challenges for social development during adolescence. Along with physical and cognitive development, adolescents experience changing school environments and changing societal expectations, limitations, and opportunities (e.g., regarding curfews, transportation, employment, dating, voting, substance use). Secondary education students are in the process of changing social roles, from children to adolescents, and ultimately of being defined by society, and by themselves, as young adults.

As a result of these changing roles, parents and teachers might expect greater independence and responsibility in adolescent students—or conversely, might resist such independence. Students might similarly expect or resist greater independence. Peers can have a greater impact on decisions adolescents consider personal, such as what to wear, whom to associate with, and how to spend free time. However, adults often continue to influence decisions that involve moral or conventional considerations (Smetana & Bitz, 1996), especially if strong, positive adult–adolescent relationships are established and maintained. These relationships strongly influence the selection and quality of peer relationships. These peer groups in turn influence the later development of deeper friendships and romantic relationships (Collins & Laursen, 2004a, 2004b).

As adolescents experience these social changes, they often encounter social challenges as well. How should they interact with adult authorities as they begin to approach adulthood themselves? How should they interact with peers as social opportunities and expectations begin to change, including opportunities for adult-like intimacy in friendships, dating, and sexuality? Educators can play an important role in helping students respond to these changing social opportunities appropriately in the context of school environments. Specifically, educators can provide opportunities for healthy social interaction within and outside the classroom, guidelines for appropriate social interaction in various contexts (e.g., classroom interactions, hallways, lunchrooms, before and after school, sports activities, dances), and specific instruction in social skills relevant to these contexts.

Each of the developmental areas mentioned above—physical, cognitive, and social—involve changes, and these changes have implications for educational practice. In Table 2.1 we summarize a few examples of changes associated with each of these developmental areas, along with some suggestions for educators. These examples might be considered a starting point for further discussion of the relationship between developmental issues and educational practices.

DEVELOPMENTAL INTERACTIONS

Interactions between physical, cognitive, and social development can result in several additional areas of development that adolescents might navigate more or less successfully. Our discussion of three areas in which adolescents might face additional challenges should not be considered exhaustive, but points to some of the challenges that might emerge in these areas in the context of secondary education environments. These considerations are especially important in planning interventions and preventive activities for improving social and behavioral functioning, and gaining an awareness of unique opportunities and challenges that might be encountered in secondary education contexts.

TABLE 2.1. Developmental Changes during Adolescence and Suggestions for Educators

Developments	Changes occurring	Suggestions for educators
Physical	Students experience rapid growth, changes in physical appearance, changing hormone levels, varying development rates, etc.	Educators can ensure the physical and emotional safety of students (e.g., prevent bullying, teach social skills, reinforce positive behaviors), provide information, healthy nutrition, and opportunities for physical activity.
Cognitive	Brain development continues during adolescence, contributing to increases in critical thinking, information-processing speed, etc.	Educators can provide appropriate levels of cognitive challenge, link what is previously known to what is being taught, and provide clear, logical rationales for rules and expectations.
Social	Students experience changing social roles, opportunities, needs for adult guidance, and perceptions of authority; peers may become more important, and peer relationships more intimate.	Educators can support positive social development by providing social opportunities, teaching and reinforcing positive social skills, and providing clear guidelines and expectations for social interactions in school contexts.

Autonomy and Responsibility

Secondary education students are grappling with new ways of thinking, encountering new social roles, and experiencing changes in the way they look and feel. Not only do they begin to think more like adults, they begin to look and feel more like adults, and in some ways they might begin to be treated more like adults and less like children. Because these changes do not happen all at once, adolescents can struggle with balancing opportunities for increased autonomy, or self-management, and the accompanying responsibility. For example, an adolescent who has the cognitive and physical ability to drive a car without adult supervision may not yet have the ability to effectively handle social distractions when transporting peers—and may not be prepared to take responsibility either for their safety or the results of a traffic accident. Adolescents whose opportunities or desires for adult-level autonomy come before they are cognitively, socially, or physically ready for adult-level responsibilities might be perceived as behaving irresponsibly.

As adolescent students begin to rethink their roles in relation to adults and children, previously accepted school rules and adult authority may also begin to be challenged. For example, students might push back against dress codes, rules about talking out of turn, seating arrangements, rules about hall or restroom passes, or use of personal items (e.g., cell phones) in the classroom. In order to effectively respond to these challenges, educators should understand and help students understand the relationship between autonomy and responsibility. Educators should encourage students to share their perceptions and understanding of academic, social, and behavioral expectations at the school in order to understand where students may be recognizing or failing to recognize their responsibilities as well as their opportunities for autonomy or self-management. Educators can then be clearer both in describing *what* is expected and in explaining *why* it is expected in terms of shared and individual responsibilities and opportunities.

Identity and Self-Concepts

Adolescence is an important time for developing identity and self-concepts, particularly because changing social roles and cognitive abilities allow adolescents to define themselves in new ways (Harter & Monsour, 1992; Marcia, 2002). Young adolescents, especially middle or junior high students in the context of a new school, may at first feel like an outsider—unsure of what others expect, what places are safe or dangerous, or even how to meet some basic needs. New environments, along with expanding cognitive, physical, and social capabilities and challenges, can produce a sense of excitement and adventure, but also increased anxiety—or both at the same time.

Part of the anxiety students experience might result from being unsure of one's role in relation to new people, places, and opportunities. Such anxiety might result alternately in withdrawal or bravado and even aggression. The SWPBS model of tiered intervention mentioned in Chapter 1 could represent a continuum of reactions to the demands placed on students as they grapple with both developmental changes in themselves and environmental changes in schools. As the SWPBS model suggests, when appropriate levels of guidance and support are in place, most adolescents can successfully navigate the new contexts of secondary education. This high level of success points to both the resilience of adolescents and the power of supportive environments.

In addition to parents and teachers, peers can provide an added measure of support during the transitions of adolescence. In a new situation, adolescents can be naturally drawn both to those who might provide guidance, and to those who might provide emotional support. Many students, who might formerly have relied primarily on adults for both of these needs, turn increasingly to peers for emotional support as they enter this time of rapid change. If students identify with positive peer groups, this emotional support can lead to positive outcomes. Conversely, if students identify with negative peer groups (e.g., gangs), negative labels from self or others could result in lasting harmful effects on behavior. Thus, school and home environments that help adolescents affiliate with positive peer groups and develop positive self-concepts are highly desirable.

Students from minority ethnic or cultural groups may face unique challenges as they seek to define themselves in relation to their peers (Holcomb-McCoy, 2005; Phinney, 1989). These students may feel pressure not only to define themselves as adolescents in relation to adults, peers, and younger children but also as participants in a culture in which they are a minority. Feeling marginalized might bring an intense desire for identity and belonging, increasing vulnerability to social pressure. Students might also be unsure about their capability for successful autonomous functioning when faced with unfamiliar social and environmental situations. Adolescents who develop strategies to seek belonging, identity, and a certain level of independence that merge well with the new contexts they enter can experience a great deal of success. However, adolescents who develop strategies in opposition to the demands of these contexts may experience struggle and conflict.

Adolescents also begin to think of themselves in more complex ways. Social and cognitive changes allow for the emergence of different, sometimes competing, self-concepts in early adolescence. In midadolescence, students may become increasingly aware of conflicting ideas or concepts about the self, which can result in confusion and anxiety. An adolescent might feel outgoing in certain contexts (such as at a sports event), but shy and withdrawn in others (such as during a classroom discussion). These conflicts may not be reconciled until later adolescence or young adulthood when cognitive development is more advanced (Harter & Monsour, 1992).

Secondary education contexts typically supply many opportunities for the exploration of identity and the development of positive self-concepts, such as engagement in sports, clubs, academics, the arts, and so on. However, as noted, possibilities for negative self-concepts may also emerge, making it crucial for educators to not only facilitate academic competence but also social and behavioral competence and success.

Moral Awareness and Functioning

Along with trying to navigate issues of autonomy and responsibility, and exploring identity and self-concepts, adolescents increasingly encounter different perspectives about values, beliefs, and behavioral expectations. The ways in which adolescents react to these perspectives (e.g., challenge, thoughtful consideration, acceptance) may arise from interactions between the physical, cognitive, and social changes they are experiencing, and their interpretation of these changes. For example, physical development might create shifts in whether students feel vulnerable or powerful in relation to others, changing social roles might increase awareness of competing demands or expectations, and cognitive development might allow students to more fully understand or effectively challenge the perspectives of others.

Thus, views on what constitute appropriate behaviors and behavior rationales may undergo changes during adolescence. Some behaviors once considered moral or as part of society's conventions may be seen as part of the adolescent's personal domain—subject to peer influence and individual decision making. This shifting of how behaviors are understood and defined can involve reconsideration of moral and conventional expectations or rules, sometimes resulting in conflict with adult authorities (Smetana & Bitz, 1996). For example, if a teacher thinks that interrupting others or talking out of turn has moral (e.g., disrespect) or conventional (e.g., impoliteness) ramifications, and a student thinks that choosing when to speak, how to speak, and whom to speak with is mostly a personal matter, a conflict might emerge.

In order to improve adolescents' social and behavioral functioning it is crucial for secondary educators to understand student perspectives on social and behavioral issues or conflicts, and on relevant concepts such as fairness, civility, or respect. Simply demanding respect without understanding how students might interpret respect can undermine the efforts of educators to facilitate moral functioning in their students. Once students and educators come to an understanding of the relevant issues, educators can be clearer in defining behavioral expectations and providing rationales that are meaningful for students.

Table 2.2 outlines a few of the issues students might face in navigating autonomy and responsibility, identity and self-concepts, and moral awareness and functioning (middle column). As with Table 2.1, some suggestions for educators are outlined in the right column as a starting point for further discussion. In the next section we explore how secondary educational contexts might either encourage or inhibit successful navigation of the challenges of adolescence as students also encounter the challenges of working with others in educational settings.

TABLE 2.2. Developmental Interactions during Adolescence and Suggestions for Educators

Interactions	Issues	Suggestions for educators
Autonomy and responsibility	Adolescents are navigating adult, peer, and personal expectations regarding autonomy and responsibility as they develop physically and cognitively.	Educators can clearly define adult and student responsibilities, teach self-management, and increase student participation in educational decisions.
Identity and self-concepts	Adolescents are exploring new roles and opportunities, trying to making sense of emerging self-concepts, and making initial commitments to an identity.	Educators can provide opportunities for safe exploration of social and occupational roles while facilitating social, academic, and behavioral competence.
Moral awareness and functioning	Adolescents become aware of different perspectives on values, beliefs, and behavioral expectations, and may challenge, thoughtfully consider, or accept alternative views.	Educators can clearly define expectations, encourage students to share their perspectives, and provide rationales for behavioral expectations that are meaningful to students.

STRENGTHS AND CHALLENGES
OF SECONDARY EDUCATION CONTEXTS

As students move into middle or junior high school, they may encounter a bewildering array of changes in their immediate educational environment. For example, in elementary school most students spent much of the day in one class with one teacher; now they need to acclimate to multiple classrooms and teachers, varied teaching styles and expectations, different content specialties, and thus social contexts that vary throughout the day. Secondary educational environments may represent both challenges and opportunities for facilitating healthy adolescent development.

> **As students move into middle or junior high school, they may encounter a bewildering array of changes in their immediate educational environment.**

Opportunities and Choices

Secondary educational contexts can provide important opportunities for students to grow in each of these areas if environments are compatible with the physical, cognitive, and social needs of growing adolescents. New opportunities for engaging in sports, clubs, student government, and other social activities may be provided, along with increased opportunities to engage at a deeper intellectual level in academic specialties, the arts, or other interest areas.

In addition to facilitating physical, social, and intellectual development, these opportunities may allow students opportunities for increased autonomy, identity exploration, and more mature moral functioning. Secondary students have more choice in which activities they want to join, when to participate, and how intensely to become involved. They also have the opportunity to try on roles in which they might become a part of the broader school community. For example, rather than simply having a time of day devoted to physical education, drawing, and writing, students may encounter opportunities to *become* basketball players, artists, or writers, and to belong to a group that shares similar interests or talents. Students may also be given a larger role in participating in the development of rules, expectations, and consequences. With an adequate level of guidance and support, many students thrive in such a setting.

Misfits and Conflicts

However, these opportunities may become challenges for students who are not well prepared for such changes or when individual differences in developmental needs are not taken into account. With the transition to secondary school, many students can experience decreased interest and motivation along with lower academic achievement. Truancy and other problem behaviors may also increase. Researchers investigating these problems suggest that such difficulties may emerge when there is a misfit between educational practices and the specific developmental needs of students (Eccles, 2004; Eccles et al., 1993).

There are several areas that have been identified in which educators may fail to adequately address the developmental needs of students entering secondary educational contexts:

- Teacher beliefs and expectations.
- Teacher control and student autonomy.
- Teacher–student relationships.
- Instructional climate.

The remainder of this section addresses ways in which a misfit between educational practices and developmental needs in these four areas might present barriers to academic, social, or behavioral success for some students. Possible solutions are also explored. Subsequent chapters provide more detail on educational practices that facilitate social, academic, and behavioral success for students with different levels of need. As these areas of possible conflict are identified, educators may come to view misbehavior not as simply a problem with the student's development but as a challenge to positively impact student behavior through effective educational practices.

Teacher Beliefs and Expectations

Teacher beliefs and expectations about both the abilities of students and the value of what is taught are important to student achievement, especially when students adopt these beliefs and expectations as their own (Bouchey & Harter, 2005). When students accept high expectations (e.g., the belief that all students can learn and improve), their learning tends to increase as they develop a sense of confidence, competence, and connectedness to teachers and to their school. In contrast, when teachers lack confidence in students' abilities to learn or their own ability to teach, students are more likely to feel alienated, to disengage, and to experience negative emotions (e.g., a sense of helplessness). These students feel neither belonging nor significant autonomy in school settings. They may exhibit their needs in ways not conducive to learning (Eccles, 2004).

> **Teacher beliefs and expectations about both the abilities of students and the value of what is taught are important to student achievement, especially when students adopt these beliefs and expectations as their own.**

Unfortunately, lower self-efficacy in teachers tends to be more common in middle and junior high school than in elementary settings, and in schools that serve more ethnic minority and fewer affluent students (Eccles, 2004). This decrease in self-efficacy suggests a mismatch between student needs and teacher expectations. When students are most likely to feel unsettled, unsure, and anxious, they may encounter teachers whose doubts about their own efficacy as teachers may result in diminished expectations for students' academic, social, or behavioral success. These diminished expectations may seem to confirm adolescent uncertainties. Often this feeling is more pronounced for students from diverse ethnic or low socioeconomic backgrounds. Research also indicates that girls are more likely to face low teacher expectations in math and science, and boys may face low expectations for their social skills and behavior. Students facing a level of uncertainty with their developmental changes may be particularly sensitive and susceptible to what they perceive teachers expect—positive or negative. Teacher expectations, regarding their own success as teachers as well as that of their students, can then become self-fulfilling prophecies insofar as students believe them and act them out (Eccles).

Teacher Control and Student Autonomy

Perhaps related to low expectations for student achievement, many secondary teachers tend to be more concerned about controlling or managing student behavior than are elementary educators (Eccles, 2004). If methods of classroom management tend to overly restrict student autonomy (e.g., punitive approaches), another mismatch may arise between students' developmental needs and the instructional environments—especially if students have less autonomy than they had in elementary school. Many elementary schools provide opportunities for unstructured playtime, such as recess; involve hands-on discovery-based learning activities; and allow for frequent activity changes to match student interest and attention levels. Secondary students may be assumed to have longer attention spans and greater ability to stay on task, resulting in more lecture-based instruction through which they are expected to remain quiet, relatively immobile, and focused for long periods of time. Even physical education may be highly structured in comparison with elementary settings. If teachers are not responsive to students' interests and needs, these changing demands may be perceived as a loss of autonomy, contributing to a student's sense of marginalization in the new secondary school context—possibly extending to student disengagement, decreased motivation, and strained student–teacher relationships.

However, if secondary educators facilitate appropriate levels of student autonomy by inviting students to participate in classroom decision making and giving students the tools to successfully manage their own behavior, teachers and students may both benefit. For example, Cade, a consistently disruptive student in a junior high social skills class, appeared to have a strong influence on others in the class. Several classmates liked him, and if he acted out they were likely to follow. After one particularly disruptive episode, the teacher did not send the student to the office as usual, but pointed out to him privately his ability to influence others. The teacher explained how this ability might be used to improve the classroom climate. With this compliment and suggestion, Cade became open to discussing how he might use his influence in positive ways. His teacher emphasized that it was ultimately his choice

> **To the extent that students are taught and expected to successfully manage their own academic and social behavior, they may experience greater levels of social and academic success, feel more connected to the school community, and successfully navigate the adolescent desire for increased autonomy.**

to use his ability for destructive or constructive purposes. Pleased that his ability and his autonomy were acknowledged, Cade accepted the challenge, committed to make a change, and improved his social interactions in the classroom. His academic performance also notably improved.

To the extent that students are taught and expected to successfully manage their own academic and social behavior, they may experience greater levels of social and academic success, feel more connected to the school community, and successfully navigate the adolescent desire for increased autonomy. Teachers can worry less about management and in the long term spend less time managing problem behaviors.

Teacher–Student Relationships

Positive relationships between teachers and students are associated with better student motivation, engagement, and success in academic endeavors. One particularly important component of positive teacher–student relationships is students' perception that their teachers are caring and emotionally supportive (Eccles, 2004). Another important component is a positive teacher expectation for student success. Student achievement is more likely to be high when teachers feel that their subject is important and their students are capable of learning it—*and* when students recognize and adopt these beliefs (Bouchey & Harter, 2005). When teachers hold and communicate high expectations, students are not only more likely to succeed academically, but also more likely to feel a sense of belonging at school. Positive relationships between educational personnel and students provide a crucial foundation for any effort to facilitate students' developmental, behavioral, and academic success.

Perhaps inseparable from a positive relationship with adults is a student's need for positive adult role models. If a teacher fosters positive relationships with students, they will be more willing to follow the teacher as a role model. If the teacher–student relationship is poor, students may be less likely to accept the teacher as a role model. Unfortunately, if the teacher is friendly with students, but is otherwise a less than positive role model, students may also replicate negative behaviors. For example, occasionally teachers try to garner popularity with students by engaging in playful "put-downs." While some students may appreciate the relaxed attitude, increased attention, and attempt at humor, such behavior (especially if imitated) can result in hurtful exchanges and create an emotionally unsafe environment. An adolescent's emerging sense of identity may easily be damaged by put-downs from a recognized authority, even if they are intended to be playful. Also, what is fun for one student may be quite hurtful to another. To counter this sort of exchange in her classroom, one teacher created an environment where "pull-ups" (compliments) rather than "put-downs" (criticisms) were modeled, encouraged, and rewarded. Positive relationships were fostered in an atmosphere that was also emotionally safe—and probably more fun.

As with other aspects of instructional environment, researchers have found that student perceptions of a positive relationship with teachers and an accompanying sense of belonging often decline as adolescents move into secondary schools (Eccles, 2004). Part of this decline may come from leaving the context of one-teacher/one-classroom for a situation with multiple teachers, varied expectations, more complex expectations, and more dominant peer groups. However, even with these constraints, secondary teachers seem quite capable of becoming aware of the particular needs of individual students when provided with the necessary tools and information (Caldarella, Young, Richardson, Young, & Young, 2008; Richardson, Caldarella, Young, Young, & Young, 2009). Secondary education contexts also have the advantage of multiple observers. If one teacher fails to recognize potentially problematic patterns of behavior, another teacher may notice them if vigilance is emphasized to some extent at the school and there is adequate communication among education personnel.

Instructional Climate

Research suggests that adolescent students may be less adequately served than their younger counterparts when it comes to instruction in academic, social, and behavioral concerns. Perceived relevance of content and sufficient cognitive challenge are two aspects of instructional climate that might be particularly important to consider when trying to meet developmental needs at the secondary level (Eccles, 2004). Adolescents increase in the ability and desire to link their life experiences in meaningful ways as they are making significant cognitive gains.

Too often students do not perceive secondary-level instruction as relevant to their needs or interests. Researchers report that adolescents feel bored and disengaged much of the time in secondary classrooms

> **Too often students do not perceive secondary-level instruction as relevant to their needs or interests.**

(Eccles, 2004). Teachers may dread the question "When am I ever going to need this?" and fail to answer it to the satisfaction of many adolescent students. For example, when a university supervisor asked a group of student teachers in the area of mathematics how they would answer the above question, they responded that they didn't know when students might use higher levels of mathematics unless their students were planning to become math teachers. This suggests not only that these student teachers were unprepared to help students link mathematics meaningfully to their lives, but that these student teachers—math education majors—were themselves having difficulty finding relevance for higher mathematics outside the classroom. If the instruction students are getting does not seem relevant to their meaningful interests, students may not invest in learning beyond trying to get a grade.

However, when teachers help students find personal relevance in instructional content, both interest and achievement can be enhanced. Having barely survived high school mathematics, Mike (mentioned in the vignette at the beginning of the chapter) strenuously avoided math in college until an art professor helped him to see the importance of math for both visual art and music—two of his longtime interests. This connection eventually helped him successfully navigate (and even sometimes enjoy) the statistics courses required for an academic career in the social sciences.

Instruction at the secondary level may also sometimes fail to account for students' emerging cognitive abilities. In some cases environments in elementary school may be more cognitively challenging than those in secondary school—particularly if secondary education teachers neglect the creative application, questioning, and exploration that are often part of elementary instruction and rely more on simple memorization of facts (Eccles, 2004; Eccles et al., 1993). For example, some secondary educators might assume that paste and paint are more appropriate for an elementary context. However, after finding that his students expected high school history to be boring, one teacher encouraged some of them to build model World War II airplanes and then develop a presentation about the airplanes for the class. These students took ownership of the project, and their growing interest in the airplanes, and desire to give a good presentation to their peers, led them to discover facts about World War II that the teacher had not encountered until college.

> **After finding that his students expected high school history to be boring, one teacher encouraged some of them to build model World War II airplanes and then develop a presentation about the airplanes for the class.**

Student workloads might also increase as students move into secondary contexts where they must respond to the expectations of multiple teachers, who may be unaware of the total demands on individual students. This increase in workload might create an illusion of greater intellectual rigor when the reality might simply be more time consumed by "busywork." Students are particularly frustrated when their grades drop, due more to boredom or exhaustion than to inability.

Because of the rapid growth and physical changes they experience, adolescents typically need almost nine hours of sleep each night (Dahl & Hariri, 2005), and should pay particular attention to good nutrition. Unfortunately, with the increased demands on their time, too many students sleep less and eat more thoughtlessly during adolescence than during periods of more moderate physical growth. With unmet physical needs, excessive academic workloads, and a perceived irrelevance of course content, some students react by disengaging, acting out, or becoming involved in unproductive activities that do not contribute to healthy development.

Fortunately, a great many problems can be avoided by emphasizing manageable and meaningful instruction, fostering positive teacher–student relationships, and increasing student autonomy in a supportive environment. As students and teachers begin to see more academic, social, and behavioral success, teacher beliefs and expectations may also improve, leading in turn to greater student success. As secondary educators become aware of the challenges and developmental needs that adolescents are experiencing, solutions may also become more apparent.

> **A great many problems can be avoided by emphasizing manageable and meaningful instruction, fostering positive teacher–student relationships, and increasing student autonomy in a supportive environment.**

SCHOOLS, COMMUNITIES, AND ADOLESCENT BELONGING

Classroom environments are embedded in larger communities both within and beyond the school setting (Eccles, 2004). If there is some level of schoolwide consistency in classroom management, resulting consistency in classroom environments may lead to a more unified school climate and community, and thus to greater security and better adjustment of students. But if students encounter broadly different approaches across classrooms and grades, they may have more difficulty understanding how they fit in these different contexts and what is expected of them. Some of this variation is, of course, inevitable and even desirable. However, creating a consistent sense of shared expectations is reasonable, and has been accomplished in many schools. Teachers, administrators, counselors, and other school professionals can work together to facilitate transitions between classrooms and grades insofar as they are aware of where challenges might exist for students at various ages and developmental levels.

If schools seek to develop both a strong sense of cooperative community within the school and positive links to the wider surrounding communities, students may feel less anxiety and isolation as they move from elementary to secondary contexts. Secondary educators may also be better able to help students make meaningful links between academic, social, and behavioral expectations across classrooms and between school, home, and a wider community. Such meaningful links could increase instructional relevance and decrease busywork. A sense of community within the school can be fostered as faculty and staff work together to create a positive, safe, and engaging school environment, develop clear and common expectations for themselves and for their students, and consistently follow through with these expectations in effective ways.

As schools work toward creating a sense of community within the school, as well as continuity with the broader community, students will likely experience familiarity and continuity as well. This familiarity, continuity, and community can help adolescents gain a sense of belonging and identity, which is foundational for successfully increasing autonomy and responsibility. Having a sense that they belong to a larger community, students will feel more confident to take initiative and engage with this community in meaningful ways. Awareness of this larger community is a first step toward improving the overall school climate, which is discussed in more detail in the following chapter.

SUMMARY

We began this chapter by describing some of the changes that occur during adolescence in physical, cognitive, and social development. Interactions between these areas of development can influence adolescents to seek more autonomy, explore identities and self-concepts, and increase their awareness of moral perspectives and functioning. Suggestions were given for how teachers might respond to these developmental changes and interactions in order to facilitate positive adolescent development. We then explored some of the strengths and challenges of educational contexts, noting that these contexts may provide both developmental opportunities and conflicts between educational practices and students' developmental needs. Drawing on Eccles's (2004) research in this area, we specifically addressed how conflicts might emerge when educators have low expectations about their abilities to influence their students, or of their students' abilities to succeed; when teachers overly restrict student autonomy rather than providing opportunities for self-management; when teacher–student relationships are poor; and when instructional climates do not meet students' needs. Finally, we emphasized that gaining an awareness of, and addressing students' developmental needs in the wider contexts of the school and community may facilitate transitions to secondary education contexts and a sense of cooperation and community within the school.

CHAPTER 3

The Importance of School Climate

Travis, an eighth-grade student, is having difficulty adjusting to life in middle school. When Travis's father got a new job, the family had to move to a new town, and Travis is having trouble making friends and fitting in. After some teasing by older boys about being the "new freak in town," and the humiliation of having food thrown at him in lunchroom, Travis strikes out and hits one of these boys in plain sight of the school's assistant principal. Travis is promptly escorted to the office, school disciplinary proceedings are initiated, and he is suspended from school. When he tries to explain his situation, the principal tells Travis that the school has a strict "zero-tolerance" policy for such behavior and that he should have considered other ways to solve his peer problems before hitting another student.

Travis's situation is all too common, as secondary schools often have a range of aversive elements that can contribute to unsafe and unhealthy environments. In schools across the United States, increased security measures and strict disciplinary policies are often implemented. Metal detectors and increased school security personnel are perceived as efficient solutions to increasing school aggression. These strategies tend to be reactive and punitive, with police officers often replacing educators in maintaining order in schools. How do these approaches affect school climate? What is school climate and why is it important? How does school climate influence the behavior of students and adults? What can be done to improve school climate?

UNDERSTANDING SCHOOL CLIMATE

There are several definitions for the term *school climate*; it can be broadly defined as characteristics that distinguish one school from another and influence the behavior of those involved with the school (Hoy & Hannum, 1997). Such breadth is justified, as the concept is as much social and psychological as physical. School climate includes the following characteristics:

- Physical aspects of the school facilities.
- Programs and resources available to students and staff.

- Instructional management strategies.
- School leadership practices.
- Parent and teacher support.
- Relationships of staff, students, and the community.

As adults, we realize that work environments influence job performance: The same principles apply to school environments for youth (Deal & Peterson, 2009). Most of us have had experiences with a work environment that was unpleasant, tiresome, or annoying. Maybe the boss was demanding and sharp or coworkers were hostile and unfriendly. Typically, we try to escape or avoid these environments by going to work late, finding excuses to leave early, or reacting in defensive, irritable ways. We are neither confident nor motivated to do our best work. Students similarly seek to escape and avoid aversive school climates; their academic outcomes suffer, and relationships feel negative.

Characteristics of a Healthy School Climate

An individual who visits a number of secondary schools may notice a different "feeling" or tone in the various schools. Some feel safe and inviting; perhaps the teachers and students appear positive, friendly, and outgoing. The school seems like a place where students and teachers want to be (Hansen & Childs, 1998). This is the ambiance of a positive school climate. Cohen (2007) identified some essential dimensions of a healthy school climate with sample indicators of what these might look like in a school:

- Safety
  - Students are taught respectful, civil, friendly behaviors over time, which are explicitly reinforced by school adults.
  - School adults emphasize positive behaviors rather than focusing only on consequences for inappropriate behaviors.
  - School adults emphasize clear rules and consequences regarding verbal abuse, harassment, and teasing; people feel safe in the school; a school safety plan is in place.
- Teaching and learning
  - High expectations exist for student learning.
  - Students are provided help when needed.
  - School adults frequently use praise and rewards.
  - Development of social, emotional, and ethical learning is emphasized.
  - School leadership communicates a clear and compelling vision.
- Professional development
  - Training is systematic, ongoing, and based on survey data from teachers and ODR data.
  - Teachers feel their professional development activities are important.
- Relationships
  - Respect for diversity is integrated into the school culture.
  - Positive relationships exist at the school (between and among both adults and students).
  - Decision making is shared.

○ A sense of community exists within the school.
○ Parents participate in school decision making and the establishment of school norms.
- Environment
  ○ The school is clean and has adequate facilities, space, teaching materials, and time to accomplish its mission.

Approaching a school with a healthy climate, a visitor would notice that the facilities are well maintained, there is no litter, and the grounds are kept clean and organized. The school seems open and inviting. By the main entrance the school colors and the school mascot are proudly displayed. Along with athletic trophies, there are pictures of students with a variety of accomplishments: a student participating in a music competition, a student winning a martial arts tournament, a group of students celebrating a service-learning experience. In the main hallways is a teacher "Hall of Fame," with pictures and stories of teachers with special accomplishments or recognition, including testimonials from students highlighting ways teachers have been a positive influence for them. Other walls could be filled with quotes from faculty and passages from literature, and a very prominent space is provided for recognizing students'

> **Approaching a school with a healthy climate, a visitor would notice that the facilities are well maintained, there is no litter, and the grounds are kept clean and organized.**

achievements and special events. Inside the office is a school mural, a signed baseball bat, and a varied collection of objects that represent interesting stories and events. Students think this is an interesting and upbeat place to be. The office is not just a place of punishment; many students come for teaching and learning, and students who are performing and progressing receive praise.

Personnel at this school believe it is important to invest in students. People are willing to take risks and are not satisfied with doing what has always been done. Teachers are appreciated through recognition and activities. Teachers are provided with professional development opportunities and an established structure and time to meet and collaborate in professional communities. The principal has established connections with the local university whereby professors make visits for guest lectures and presentations. Other university faculty members have worked with the teachers in the school to improve the curriculum and establish a variety of activities. Students are taught and mentored by teachers and other educators in the school.

Are there problems? Yes. Do the administrators and teachers feel like this is the perfect school? No. They are well aware of the underachievement of some students, highlighted by the required state achievement tests. Some teachers complain about the administration, and some administrators complain about some teachers. While parents are an integral part of the organization, some do not feel included and others may not feel that their concerns are being addressed. But most members of the school community have participated in and are committed to continual improvement of the learning environment. Although weaknesses are systematically identified and addressed, there are some problems that baffle the administration and

> **The school is a place of support and courage, a place where teachers and students want to be.**

teachers when reasonable interventions do not seem to work. The school is a place of support and courage, a place where teachers and students *want* to be (Hansen & Childs, 1998).

Drawbacks of a Reactive and Punitive Approach

The traditional response to student misbehavior in secondary schools has been in-school punishment (which typically includes time out, chastisement, loss of privileges, and detention), suspension, or expulsion. Corporal punishment in schools (e.g., spanking, paddling) is still legal

> **Punitive, reactive discipline is often viewed as harsh and unfeeling, and students tend to respond with anger and fear.**

in some parts of the United States (Jacob & Hartshorne, 2007) and unfortunately still occurs at high rates (Society for Adolescent Medicine, 2003). Such coercive approaches to managing behavior hinder rather than encourage a healthy school climate and have been noted to result in a variety of negative side effects (Sidman, 1989). For example, punitive, reactive discipline is often viewed as harsh and unfeeling, and students tend to respond with anger and fear. Some students attempt to escape or avoid future interactions with the punisher. Others engage in more extreme reactions: vandalism, aggression, or antisocial behavior (Walker, Ramsey, & Gresham, 2004). When punishment is predominant in a school, students may adopt an attitude of "What can I do without being caught?" Zero-tolerance policies tend to be punitive, and administrators have little choice in responding to complex situations because the policy requires that students be expelled or suspended without consideration of the broader context of the behavior. While such strategies may temporarily stop the misbehavior, they do not teach appropriate replacement behaviors, nor do they contribute to a positive school climate (Walker et al.).

Other reactive approaches include increased monitoring and get-tough policies. For example, surveillance cameras, metal detectors, electronic-card-entry devices, and security guards are popularly used to reduce aggressive or bullying behavior, but they may not create safer schools. Surveillance cameras or other security devices may be constant reminders to students that they are in a hostile or unsafe environment. School climate is negatively affected when these precautions send a message that the environment and the students themselves are not trustworthy, and that such tactics are needed to keep the school safe (Kitsantas, Ware, & Martinez-Arias, 2004).

> **When punishment is predominant in a school, students may adopt an attitude of "What can I do without being caught?"**

Punitive reactions also tend to influence academic outcomes: students who are suspended or expelled are likely to suffer academically as they miss classroom instruction. Federal or state legal mandates may require suspension and expulsion in some serious situations, and these situations are non-negotiable in most instances. But if school personnel default to the reactive, punitive responses for *all* misbehavior, or rely on these approaches without also making preventative efforts, school climate will be negatively affected. Punitive strategies do not facilitate positive relationships that focus on working together to fix mistakes, learn new behaviors, and make restitution for hurtful actions. Additionally, punishment does not offer opportunities for teaching and reinforcing positive behaviors. Get-tough, zero-tolerance policies function as quick fixes to stop serious behaviors and send messages to the school community that violence and aggression will not be permitted, but they are likely to lead to a negative, hostile school community that lacks trust. Students tend to feel less safe in this type of environment, and these insecure feelings lead to a negative school climate, which does not contribute to positive student outcomes.

The fear of punishment, which is at the heart of reactive approaches, has the potential to discourage students and teachers from taking preventive actions when faced with potential problems. For example, more than 20 students and at least one teacher were aware of a California student's threats to "shoot up" his school the day before he did so. Nobody took his threats seriously, and some told reporters that they had not wanted to get their friend expelled from school for what were most likely idle threats (Chapin & Gleason, 2004). The fear of punishment rather than a sense of mutual caring, trust in decision makers, and teamwork in solving problems was dominant at this school.

> **The fear of punishment, which is at the heart of reactive approaches, has the potential to discourage students and teachers from taking preventive actions when faced with potential problems.**

Benefits of a Healthy School Climate

The benefits of developing a healthy school climate include increases in student academic achievement, decreases in student misbehavior, and improvements in student social and emotional well-being. Below is a summary of some of the key research findings in this area.

Effects on Student Academic Performance

- A healthy school climate helps students feel safe and cared for by adults and peers. Relationships of trust with others at school are evident, and academic performance improves (Samdal, Wold, & Bronis, 1999).
- In schools with a healthy school climate, students indicate that they put more effort into their schoolwork, are expected to perform at a higher academic level, and have higher aspirations to graduate and go on to college (Brand, Felner, Seitsinger, Burns, & Bolton, 2008).
- Healthy school climates have been linked with improvements in standardized test scores, reading levels, academic writing, and grade-point average (GPA; Garrison, 2004).

Effects on Student Behavior

- School disciplinary referrals, absences, and suspensions have been shown to be lower in schools with a healthy school climate (Haynes, Emmons, & Ben-Avie, 1997).
- When students feel connected to their school, they are more likely to confide in their teachers (Brookmeyer, Fanti, & Henrich, 2006).
- Student delinquency, aggression, antisocial behavior, and drug use are less likely to occur where there is a supportive school climate (Brand et al., 2008).

Effects on Student Well-Being

- Student aspirations, ambitions, willingness to participate, and self-confidence were higher in schools where students perceived a more supportive school climate (Plucker, 1998).
- Self-esteem and depression problems are lower for schools with a positive school climate (Brand et al., 2008).
- The school's value system and the teachers' attitudes toward students have a significant

impact on students' optimism and ability to cope, as well as their psychological and physiological well-being (Ruus et al., 2007).

Additional Benefits

- A healthy school climate is a necessary foundation for successful school reform or school improvement projects (Sterbinsky, Ross, & Redfield, 2006).
- A supportive school climate leads to a better work environment for staff and higher levels of teacher job satisfaction (Grayson & Alvarez, 2008).
- School climate has been shown to be a significant element in school improvement in low socioeconomic areas and to be particularly effective in helping disadvantaged children succeed (Muijs, Harris, Chapman, Stoll, & Russ, 2004).

The importance of improving the school climate is also evident in policy decisions and program designs. For example, of the 10 reform recommendations given by the National Research Council (2004) for engaging schools, four were directly linked to school climate. If developing a healthy school climate is a priority for successful, effective schools, both students and faculty are likely to reap a wide variety of benefits. Indeed it could be said that nothing of much lasting value can be achieved unless schools cultivate such climates. Having explored the importance of establishing a healthy school climate, this chapter now discusses ways it can be fostered in secondary schools.

FOSTERING A HEALTHY SCHOOL CLIMATE

Teachers can impact school climate, with the largest effect coming from their individual interactions and relationships with students. Positive relationships can be particularly important during adolescence, when youth are experiencing many new demands from parents, peers, teachers, and local culture.

> **Teachers can impact school climate, with the largest effect coming from their individual interactions and relationships with students.**

Positive Personal Relationships

Students who are at risk frequently have an increased need for such positive relationships, even though their attitudes and behaviors may present many challenges for a potential mentor. There are a variety of behaviors that teachers can use to help promote more positive relationships with students (Young et al., 2008), potentially resulting in an improved classroom and school climate—some of these are highlighted in Table 3.1.

Positive Classroom Management

Classroom management practices can also impact school climate. A teacher who relies on criticism and punishment to manage the classroom creates a negative classroom climate. Such behaviors frequently result in reactions of hostility, fear, and escape or avoidance by students. In contrast, managing behavior through the use of positive discipline strategies creates a safer,

TABLE 3.1. Ways to Foster Positive Interpersonal Relationships with Students

Verbal behaviors	Nonverbal behaviors
Offer to help	Use a calm, pleasant voice
Compliment and praise specific behaviors	Use pleasant facial expressions
Express concern	Spend time together
Be polite	Seek opportunities to interact
Get right to the point	Be open to concerns or criticism
Ask for help or advice	Work alongside each other
Use humor that has no put-downs or ridicule	Attend important school events

more pleasant learning environment in which students want to participate. Examples of positive classroom management practices that can result in an improved school climate include the following:

- Set high expectations for students.
- Establish and post three to five positively stated classroom rules.
- Develop and consistently implement consequences that fit the expectations.
- Emphasize positive and natural consequences, using negative consequences judiciously.
- Focus on teaching and reteaching appropriate behaviors.
- Set and maintain appropriate boundaries (behaviors that are unacceptable under any circumstances).

High-Quality Teaching

The quality of teaching in a school can also impact school climate. Boring lectures with little meaningful student involvement negatively affect the classroom climate. Poor teaching that permeates a school can affect the climate of the entire school. In contrast, quality teaching characterized by a relevant and developmentally appropriate curriculum with clear goals and strategic assessments that inform instruction creates a positive classroom learning environment (Kaplan & Owings, 2002) that can eventually extend schoolwide.

School effectiveness is greatly influenced by teachers who are dedicated and skilled, work in teams, and exhibit positive morale and enthusiasm for teaching (Townsend, 1997). Teachers who utilize class time effectively, keep students on task, and provide students with extra help also have higher-achieving students (Heck, 2000). Teachers with reasonable expectations are also an important and consistent predictor of student achievement (Samdal et al., 1999).

School Leadership

Research suggests that school leadership has a strong and direct influence on school climate. Some of the research findings connecting leadership practices and school climate are listed below.

- Students who trust those in administrative positions are less likely to commit violent acts (Anderman, 2002).
- Principals who show consistency in their leadership approach tend to have teachers who report higher levels of positive school climate (Kelley, Thornton, & Daugherty, 2005).
- Clear communication by principals has been linked with improved school climate (Halawah, 2005).
- Developing a student-centered mission, strengthening elements of the existing climate, adding new traditions and values, hiring and socializing staff to uphold and contribute to school values, and integrating school values in activities and programs have been shown to promote a healthy climate (Deal & Peterson, 1999).
- Defining and conveying the school's mission and goals help to promote a healthy climate (Witziers, Bosker, & Kruger, 2003).
- Providing individual support and contributing to the professional development of teachers are important factors in leadership (Leithwood et al., 2007), and may improve school climate.
- Leaders foster a positive school climate by respecting students and having open-door policies. Evaluating administrator practices using results-based assessment and incorporating a profit sharing system may be ways to improve school climate (Murphy & Pimentel, 1996).

Effective leaders communicate to stakeholders the goals and mission of the school and work toward a climate of collaboration involving all in responsibility for students' success. Stakeholders such as students, parents, and teachers must be recognized for their important influence in the school change process; these groups can each facilitate or inhibit efforts to bring about an improved school climate. The need for cooperation and collaboration among stakeholders requires school leaders to know where their stakeholders stand on important issues related to school climate. Stakeholders highly value a clearly articulated school purpose and a means for achieving the outcomes, especially when they have contributed to identifying the means and the anticipated outcomes. In fact, this aspect of the educational experience is critically important to teachers and parents, who tend to rate it second only to teacher quality (Townsend, 1997).

> **Effective leaders communicate to stakeholders the goals and mission of the school and work toward a climate of collaboration involving all in responsibility for students' success.**

Having a sense of the valued outcomes and stakeholder positions on these outcomes is a vital first step. Understanding the perceptions among stakeholders, especially the areas of agreement and disagreement, is also important (Richardson, Sabbah, Juchau, Caldarella, & Young, 2007). Being aware of differences in perceptions enables administrators to identify and address potential problems.

Key Leadership Practices

Building on previous research and on observations from our own work in secondary schools, we suggest four key leadership practices that contribute to a healthy school climate:

1. Purpose and direction
   - Identify and articulate a clear vision.
   - Develop and communicate school goals.
   - Motivate and inspire staff members.
   - Support high performance expectations with needed resources.
   - Promote good behavior through modeling and reinforcement.
   - Establish and practice effective communication.
2. Professional development
   - Practice distributed leadership through delegation and trust.
   - Provide meaningful incentives for teachers.
   - Use effective faculty development models that emphasize training, practice, and feedback over time.
   - Reinforce and encourage faculty members' efforts.
   - Mentor teachers and staff.
   - Adopt an open-door policy that maintains visibility.
3. Instructional management
   - Supervise and evaluate instruction.
   - Provide corrective feedback for instruction effectiveness, with reinforcement for progress.
   - Coordinate the curriculum.
   - Monitor student progress.
   - Emphasize data-based decision making.
   - Provide incentives for student and teacher learning.
   - Protect instructional time and promote quality instruction.
   - Be organized—have a clean office and an updated website.
   - Focus on prevention—prioritize and be proactive.
4. Community collaboration and cooperation
   - Invite meaningful teamwork of staff and community.
   - Respectfully respond to criticism and concerns.
   - Involve families and communities in school activities in ways that meet their needs.
   - Develop professional learning communities.
   - Obtain stakeholder buy-in and trust.
   - Have built-in, systematic, collaborative processes.
   - Build community within the school and get involved in the community outside of school.
   - Keep current on stakeholder perceptions of school practices.

Community Involvement

The most effective schools involve the entire community.

In addition to teachers and school leaders, members of the surrounding community should also be involved in developing a positive school climate. The most effective schools involve the entire community: parents, law enforcement, and mental health professionals, as well as business, religious, and other leaders. Effective schools tend to have stakeholders who perceive a positive relationship between school and home. In one study, over 90% of respondents in each class of stakeholders (parents, students, principals, and teachers) reported that positive school–home relations were very important to them, with parents valuing these relations the most; however, these participants also reported that this element needed improvement (Townsend, 1997).

Involvement of community figures makes school feel safer, which can improve school climate. When the community is supportive and involved and there are relationships of trust with teachers, administrators, and other school personnel, students are less likely to feel unsafe or to commit violent acts in school, especially when positive behavior support is practiced as well (Jacobson, 2009). Involving the community also brings more resources: a wider variety of ideas, perspectives, and problem-solving practices as well as increased physical and financial support. Such involvement communicates to students and teachers that they are not in the process of education by themselves. Having a collaborative effort tends to make problems seem more manageable.

Ways to Improve Community Involvement

Evaluating the strengths and resources available in the community can be a good first step. Involvement should be developed to maximize community resources and realistically recognize their limitations. Another important step is to gauge how the school team can involve the community. Once the community becomes involved and is actively collaborating, it is important to evaluate the effectiveness of the efforts.

Community involvement can be evaluated in a variety of ways. Perception data from school personnel, parents, and community members collected through surveys is one possibility. We have used the Indicators of School Quality (ISQ; Taylor, West, & Smith, 2006) discussed in the following section. Monitoring the use of volunteers and their reasons for volunteering is another way of understanding how community members are contributing to school climate.

We have found it helpful to encourage secondary school faculty and leaders to ask the following types of questions when addressing community involvement:

- What are administrators and teachers doing to involve the parents in instruction?
- Are school newsletters, principals' messages, or bulletins with relevant school information being sent to parents? Is there evidence that parents are reading the information and responding as needed?
- Are there opportunities for parents to volunteer in meaningful ways and to be a part of the school mission?
- Do parents know and endorse the vision and goals of the school?
- Are there opportunities for parents to come to the school at a time that is convenient for them?
- Are parents' concerns and ideas respectfully received and responded to in a prompt and effective manner?

MEASURING SCHOOL CLIMATE

If a secondary school is to improve school climate, there must be some way of measuring it effectively. Many measures of school climate are narrowly focused and do not include psychological and social factors. In monitoring school climate, a comprehensive measure should be used that includes both the physical aspects and the psychosocial factors involved. Elements such as the school facilities, the programs and resources available to students and staff, the instructional and leadership practices of administration, the support of parents and teachers, and the relationships of the staff, students, and community should be included.

Process

The process of measuring school climate should be simple, sustainable, and easy to interpret so that the data can be used to make needed changes. A measure of school climate should consider the viewpoints of students, teachers, and parents in order to get their differing perceptions about what is going well and what needs prompt attention. Ideally, school faculty and staff will consider the following types of questions as they select means of measuring school climate:

- Is this process something that we can manage year after year?
- Is the process burdensome for our teachers and parents?
- Are the data and results easy to interpret and understand?
- Can the changes in school climate be documented over time?
- Is the process of collecting the data and interpreting the results time consuming?

Applicable Data

One approach to measuring school climate is to incorporate data that are already being collected. Objective measures of school records, such as ODRs, GPAs, attendance, and suspensions are likely already being collected. Schools have to report outcomes from state or district tests. Other measures could also be collected that are relatively easy to account for such as resources (e.g., number of computers and other technology available to students, teaching resources), communications to parents and other members of the community (e.g., bulletins, messages), school facilities (e.g., safety issues, graffiti, vandalism), student information (e.g., number of students, class size, standardized test scores), and parent involvement (e.g., attendance at parent–teacher conferences, PTA membership). These data should be summarized and reported in clear and consistent ways so that trends are identified in a timely manner enabling problems to be solved efficiently.

In addition to the information routinely collected in a school, stakeholders' perceptions of the school are of value. Understanding the perceptions of stakeholders may assist administrators and school teams in creating targeted change within their schools. The most popular method is to conduct surveys among teachers, students, and parents. Several resources are available that can make this process sustainable, simple, and easy to interpret. In fact, some states have complementary school climate and student-engagement surveys with data processing available through the state Department of Education (California Department of Education, 2009). These surveys are validated and very useful as they also provide comparison data from other schools.

In some states complimentary training is also available to school administrators interested in administering surveys at their school. For schools that do not have the available resources in their area, there are other solutions, including the book *School Climate: Measuring, Improving and Sustaining Healthy Learning Environments* (Freiberg, 1999), which includes several methods and measurements necessary to monitor school climate.

Another suggested resource, one which the authors have used, is the ISQ produced by Utah State University's Center for the School of the Future (Taylor et al., 2006). The ISQ, which encompasses several elements, contains 30 items from seven factors that assess the quality of the school. The ISQ items are grouped into seven categories: parent support, teacher excellence, student commitment, school leadership, instructional quality, resource management, and school safety. The ISQ also incorporates a variety of perspectives, with versions of the survey completed by teachers, parents, and students. Table 3.2 shows a sample of the types of ISQ items—the actual survey items for each audience are slightly different (e.g., elementary students have the items worded for their expected vocabulary). The ISQ assessment process is relatively easy, as the survey takes just 5 minutes to complete. The surveys are processed electronically by Utah State University, and the data are reported in a signal analysis report with a color-coded snapshot of how the school is doing relative to previous years and in comparison to other similar

TABLE 3.2. Sample of Indicators of School Quality Items

Parent support
　　Parents support their child's education.
　　Parents know what happens at school.

Teacher excellence
　　Teachers care about students as individuals.
　　Teachers promote good behavior in their classrooms.

Student commitment
　　Students enjoy learning.
　　Students have pride in their school.

School leadership
　　Administration promotes good behavior at the school.
　　Administration has high expectations for all students.

Instructional quality
　　The school prepares students for adult life.
　　The school provides a quality education.

Resource management
　　The school has quality textbooks and instructional materials.
　　Students have enough extracurricular opportunities.

School safety
　　Students and staff feel safe at school.
　　The school is clean and in good repair.

schools. A sample signal analysis report that allows schools to see their progress relative to other schools can be found at the Center for the School of the Future website (*www.csf.usu.edu/isq.html*).

SWPBS AND SCHOOL CLIMATE

> While SWPBS was not specifically developed to improve school climate, when it is well implemented it can have such an effect.

A variety of models and programs have been developed to address school climate. While SWPBS was not specifically developed to improve school climate, it can have such an effect when it is implemented well. SWPBS is a framework that approaches school environment with prevention strategies: teaching positive, adaptive behaviors and social skills that are frequently and meaningfully reinforced by adults, rather than waiting for misbehavior to occur and then using punishment as a primary means of discipline. When adults are looking for appropriate student behaviors and reinforcing those behaviors, positive student–teacher relationships result. When students and teachers have mutually supportive relationships, student misbehavior tends to be managed more easily by the teachers in the classroom, thus decreasing the need for office referrals.

Focus on Prevention

SWPBS involves "a broad range of systemic and individualized strategies for achieving important social and learning outcomes while preventing problem behavior" (Sugai, 2002, p. 1). Thus SWPBS serves as an effective alternative for traditional punitive reactions to student misconduct. Within the SWPBS model, problem behaviors are viewed not as just a student problem but as an interaction between the environment and the child. Many problem behaviors are prevented by altering the environment before problems escalate, simultaneously teaching and reinforcing prosocial skills and positive behaviors.

A major component of the SWPBS model is its focus on preventing students' maladaptive and ineffective behaviors. This focus on prevention is in response to increasingly common reports of problems in schools that include theft, bullying, substance abuse, and acts of violence among students and toward teachers. Such behaviors are best prevented when the entire school supports and uses evidence-based practices (Sugai, 2002). In a school using SWPBS, behavioral expectations are clearly outlined and taught consistently to students. Once these expectations are clear, educators seek to reinforce students for following the rules rather than waiting for misbehavior to occur. Experience has shown that clear expectations and recognition of positive student behavior help improve school climate and culture, while punitive measures and reactive interventions can actually decrease students' feelings of safety in school (Kitsantas et al., 2004).

A Middle School Case Study

For over 4 years we tracked the effects of a SWPBS model on the school climate of a middle school (Caldarella, Shatzer, Gray, Young, & Young, in press). The model implemented at this school included teaching social skills schoolwide, instructing teachers to write praise notes to students, posting school rules, screening proactively for students at risk for emotional and behavioral disorders, and referring at-risk students for targeted interventions. Typically, educators implementing SWPBS measure outcomes by collecting data about office discipline ODRs. However, we tracked school data on student behavior and academic achievement, as well as two measures of school climate. These measures were also tracked at a comparison middle school that was not implementing SWPBS in order to examine differences between schools.

The evidence suggests that the SWPBS model helped decrease student behavior problems and improve the school climate. From the first to last year of our research, the SWPBS middle school experienced a 47% decrease in tardiness, a 35% decrease in absences, a 34% decrease in ODRs, and a 4% increase in GPA. With the exception of GPA, these changes were significant when compared to changes at the other middle school.

> The evidence suggests that the SWPBS model helped decrease student behavior problems and improve the school climate.

School climate was also measured over the period of 4 years by the ISQ and a supplemental teacher survey that, when combined, examined 10 elements of school climate. The SWPBS school experienced statistically significant improvement in nine of the 10 elements of school climate, with the element of school safety showing slight but not significant improvements (see Figure 3.1). The comparison school did not show statistically significant improvements in any of these elements of school climate. These results provide support for the positive impact of SWPBS on school climate.

SWPBS can be an effective method for improving school climate while reducing discipline problems at the secondary level. We have found in our review of research that schools experience an average 30–40% decrease in ODRs after SWPBS implementation (see Caldarella et al., in press). Not only are there fewer disturbances in the school but valuable classroom and administrative time can be invested in strengthening academic outcomes and other impor-

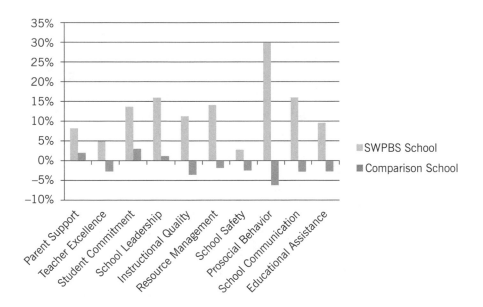

FIGURE 3.1. Percentage of change over 4 years of SWPBS for each element of school climate.

tant instructional goals. Students spend more time in the classroom and less time in detention or away from instruction, and administrators devote their time to being instructional leaders instead of disciplinarians (Black & Downs, 1993). Improved student behavior translates into improved classroom performance and improved school climate.

SUMMARY

School climate, whether or not it is directly addressed in a school, has a positive or negative impact on how well teachers teach and how well students learn. This chapter has addressed the concept of school climate: the tangible and intangible aspects that give a school its unique feel, along with some ways for specifically addressing it and implementing teacher and administrator behaviors that contribute to it. These behaviors are tied very closely to SWPBS, which can have a positive impact on school climate. When teachers and administrators become involved with SWPBS, incidents such as teasing, harassment, and bullying become teaching opportunities rather than potential tragedies.

CHAPTER 4

Planning for Implementation

During the summer Stephanie, the assistant principal at Wesley Junior High, visited her cousin Jared, an English teacher at a middle school in Illinois. She learned that many schools in that area were implementing an SWPBS model. Jared had found that the SWPBS method increased positive behavior among students (and even faculty and staff). The teachers developed a common language to discuss discipline issues among themselves and with students and parents. Behavioral expectations were clear, and teachers had common talking points when discussing problems with students or parents.

Rather than punishing students for every little problem, the building administration had become proactive in dealing with inappropriate behaviors like running in the halls and horseplay in the lunchroom. With the help of a carefully selected committee, the administrators had developed and posted positive behavioral expectations for students, such as showing respect for others, then specifically taught behaviors that showed respect—like following directions or expressing appreciation. Student behaviors were improving. The faculty frequently discussed the principles of the model, found ways to make it work in their school, and even attended some professional development the year before implementation began. Jared had thought at first that all the planning was overkill, but once the program was working, he agreed that all the groundwork had been important.

Jared believed he had developed more positive relationships with students. Rather than merely saying, "Don't talk while I am talking" or "Stop poking your neighbor," teachers were teaching acceptable behaviors and routines and trying to catch students being good; and they found they had more time for actually teaching.

Stephanie is excited about adapting and implementing this model in her school, but she has no idea what is required and how to get started. Who is responsible? How is the model sustained over time? Would the district have to be involved? How can she get the faculty of her school to agree to put in the efforts to accomplish positive change?

CREATING THE CONTEXT FOR IMPLEMENTATION

The first step in implementing SWPBS is to create a team of teachers, support personnel (e.g., counselors, school psychologists), parents, and others to assume leadership roles. Much of their initial work will be creating the context for implementation: determining needs, gathering data, planning for professional development, and gaining support of colleagues. These preliminary, time-consuming activities must be accomplished or the actual implementation will be inefficient, fragmented, and unfocused. Sustainability is more likely to occur when these foundational tasks occur. Figure 4.1 is a visual representation of creating the context for implementation.

Assembling a Planning Committee or Team

> **While the model really is quite simple—create and post positive expectations, teach positive behaviors, reinforce positive behaviors, and create a continuum of services so the needs of all students can be addressed— actually implementing it can be quite complex because there are multifaceted needs.**

Usually the team is organized a year before implementation begins, providing time to gather data and to adapt the model for the specific needs of the school. Additionally, the ideals of the model must be shared with the whole school, with consensus sought and measured. The team and all school personnel should receive training before plans become action, and resources and necessary materials should be gathered during this preimplementation year. While the model really is quite simple—create and post positive expectations, teach positive behaviors, reinforce positive

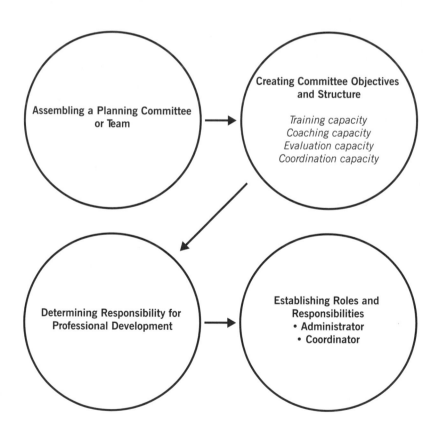

FIGURE 4.1. Creating the context for implementation.

behaviors, and create a continuum of services so the needs of all students can be addressed—actually implementing it can be quite complex because there are multifaceted needs.

To address this complexity, some teams initially focus on Tier 1 strategies (discussed in Chapter 1) and then add more intense interventions once the schoolwide or universal components are firmly in place, with data to support that predetermined outcomes are being achieved or are forthcoming. Initial focus on the universal components is highly recommended because if these universal strategies are strong and effective, students who seem to need Tier 2 interventions may really only need Tier 1 strategies. For example, because José was chronically tardy to all of his classes, he was given one day of in-school suspension and assigned to participate in a 6-week time-management class—a Tier 2 intervention. However, when the school started playing the school song during the last 30 seconds before each class begins, providing an audio prompt, José's tardies decreased from 15 each week to two. This universal intervention solved the problem: José needed additional, consistent prompting, not a 6-week time-management class.

Creating Committee Objectives and Structure

The planning committee usually addresses an overarching question or objective for the school: for example, decreasing office discipline referrals or suspensions, or increasing the students' respectful behaviors (Sugai et al., 2010). The group seeks to develop, implement, and evaluate strategies that will identify and meet the needs of all students through developing a variety of interventions that address their behavioral and emotional needs.

School teams concentrate on building four distinct school capacities (Sugai et al., 2010, p. 24):

- *Training capacity.* Use self-assessments to develop, implement, and evaluate a plan for professional development.
- *Coaching capacity.* Organize faculty/staff and other resources to adapt to the current needs and context of the school. Unlike professional development, coaching is ongoing; it focuses on implementing the training. For example, teachers may attend workshops on responding to noncompliant behaviors and then be assigned a coach to help them apply these responses in their classrooms. Coaching involves formative feedback over time as a result of observing the new strategies being used and then providing individualized support, as needed.
- *Evaluation capacity.* Utilize data to make decisions. Using school and classroom data, teams establish measurable outcomes and then use both formative and summative data to evaluate outcomes. The organizing committee develops efficient data collection systems that conserve school resources while collecting information that is reliable and meaningful.
- *Coordination capacity.* Create a system that coordinates student services to be efficient and effective. Communication is strong, clear, and timely.

Schools are likely to have several different committees that already attend to building these capacities; it is typical for schools to have a variety of committees, programs, and projects simultaneously being developed and implemented. Adding another committee to an overburdened school faculty can lead to frustration because time is typically the school's most valued yet limited resource. Administrators must first judge whether another committee is feasible. If a new committee is formed, the group should consist of about 7–10 members. A committee that is too large often becomes unwieldy, has difficulty with scheduling, and requires too much time to provide leadership. A committee that is too small may overwhelm individual members with its necessary tasks.

In some schools, an existing committee can be expanded. Current committee function and potential coordination or integration must be considered from the outset. For example, an existing discipline committee that is responsible for creating the school discipline plan or revising school rules might be expanded to include responsibility for implementing SWPBS.

An effective, efficient committee is vital to implementing this model; otherwise efforts will likely be fragmented, inconsistent, and misguided. Working with administrators, the committee articulates the new vision and the data-based goals and corrects identifiable, measurable problems such as common disrespectful behaviors or widespread discipline problems. The committee addresses the problems and creates measurable goals as it begins making decisions and planning activities. Committee efforts focus on preventing problems and responding with evidence-based practices when problems do occur, and in doing so school personnel create a common language. This communicates that positive behavior can be taught and maintained in secondary school settings.

> **An effective, efficient committee is vital to implementing this model; otherwise efforts will likely be fragmented, inconsistent, and misguided.**

Committee members should represent stakeholders in the building: both certified and noncertified staff, para-educators, parents, community members, and even students. A variety of members should be included; having a representative for each academic department (i.e., science, math, and physical education) has worked well. Later in the chapter including parents and students in this committee is addressed.

The committee is charged with adapting the core principles of SWPBS to the specific needs and context of their school and community. With input from stakeholder groups and data analysis, the committee develops objectives and expectations, and then uses data to monitor and evaluate progress. Members are advocates and guides, and as a group they should have the political power to ensure that the model is implemented. They are perceived to have expertise and know-how, and they should serve for several years in order to maintain the momentum of their efforts. Frequent changes in membership may hamper team efficiency.

Determining Responsibility for Professional Development

One function of the committee is to plan schoolwide professional development and coaching. Though not generally responsible for presenting the workshops, the members will locate speakers or skilled trainers to teach all faculty the needed skills and use data to determine what instruction is needed. Scheduling the professional development can be complicated. Some schools hire a group of substitutes to take over the language arts classes in the morning and the science classes in the afternoon, and training is by department. Professional collaboration time may be used to provide small-group instruction. As the plan is implemented, committee members may coach small groups of teachers.

Finding time and resources to adequately prepare and sustain school personnel is imperative. The authors' experience has shown that skimping on training undercuts the sustainability of the model. Insufficient teacher training made continuing the model more challenging each year. If meaningful time cannot be devoted to maintaining teacher skills, the timing may not be right to implement SWPBS.

Preservice and most inservice teacher training targets a specific emphasis such as math or science. Learning about the social, emotional, and behavioral needs of students may seem disconnected to teaching algebra or chemistry. Teaching social skills may be perceived as changing teacher roles. In some schools only special educators work with students with behavioral concerns, but this model asks all teachers to provide support and interventions to a wide variety of youth because behavior and emotional problems can impact all teaching contexts.

> **This model asks all teachers to provide support and interventions to a wide variety of youth because behavior and emotional problems can impact all teaching contexts.**

Establishing Roles and Responsibilities

As the organization and structure of the committee are established, widespread understanding of the roles and responsibilities of members and leaders is critical. When individuals comprehend and agree to their roles, they are more likely to participate in ways that facilitate the overarching objectives of the committee. Because some confusion and exploration around roles is natural, it is important to occasionally return to conversations that explicitly determine how the committee works and functions.

Administrator

The principal must be perceived by the school community as the leading advocate for the philosophy and overarching strategies of this model, although perhaps not highly involved in specific activities. Without the full support of the principal, changes in policy and procedures are likely to be temporary at best—an inefficient use of school resources. Similarly, other initiatives may squeeze committee efforts and divert needed resources unless principal support is present. The administrator's role is to prioritize SWPBS and advocate for implementation with fidelity.

Competing objectives may overcome available resources, compromising their effectiveness. The building administrator articulates how this model fits into the major objectives of the school and will assist faculty in meeting their individual and group objectives—which is consistent with the administrative responsibility for allocation and use of school resources (Batsche, n.d.). At one introductory professional development meeting a teacher expressed concern over adding one more thing to her already full plate. The understanding and supportive principal, who is highly committed to SWPBS, kindly replied, "This isn't one more thing to add to your plate. This is the plate."

One of the building administrators (e.g., one of the assistant principals) typically serves on the organizing committee, but rarely leads the meeting. By attending the meetings and reporting to the principal, the administrator helps to ensure that everyone knows what everyone else is doing, so that efforts throughout the school are coordinated and services are not being unnecessarily duplicated.

Coordinator

The committee is led by a coordinator, or committee chairperson, appointed by the administration. Although specific responsibilities vary, the coordinator is essentially responsible for overseeing the committee's guidance of the implementation process (calling meetings, ensuring that records are kept, developing the agenda, gathering resources, interpreting the data, communicating with the faculty and staff, and giving assignments) and generally being the go-to person for a wide variety of operations. No special behavior management skills are needed, but organizational skills are essential. A school counselor or school psychologist may be named as coordinator; although expertise in behavior management is not required, this individual's typically flexible schedule and awareness of needs throughout the building may be especially helpful. A classroom teacher who has time to dedicate to the tasks may serve in this position. Decreasing the teaching or caseload of the coordinator often provides benefits that justify the associated responsibilities.

Though specific professional competencies are not required for the coordinator, some personal skills are needed to facilitate committee work. Excellent communication skills, both verbal and written, are important in conveying the purpose and function of SWPBS, which is especially important during initial implementation. Organizational skills enable the coordinator to sequence the implementation process, keep information accessible, make assignments and receive reports, and conduct efficient, effective meetings. Choosing a faculty member who colleagues respect and perceive as a leader gives credibility and implied status to the efforts. Momentum will be facilitated if the coordinator serves for several years.

ACCESSING SCHOOL RESOURCES

> **Human resources include time to contribute, expertise in student behavioral and emotional issues, willingness to participate, and knowledge of community resources, in addition to leadership ability, communication skills, artistic talent, technological competency, grant-writing skills, and especially data analyses.**

Accessing resources of the school begins with identifying resources currently available. These can generally be divided into two categories: human and physical. (Figure 4.2 highlights this aspect of the process.) Human resources include time to contribute, expertise in student behavioral and emotional issues, willingness to participate, and knowledge of community resources, in addition to leadership ability, communication skills, artistic talent, technological competency, grant-writing skills, and especially data analyses. Additional personnel may be needed, or personnel may need to change focus and responsibilities. Physical resources consist of money and the things money can buy; it may also include space in the school. The supplies needed to implement are generally available in schools (copy paper and a copy machine). Depending on how the model is implemented, incentives may be required for both teachers and students.

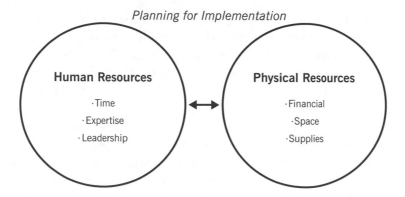

FIGURE 4.2. Accessing school resources.

Human Resources

Once the committee is organized, human resources must be identified. Including every competent individual in the building on the committee is not feasible, but many individuals outside the committee may contribute to specific projects. For example, the teacher of a self-contained classroom for children with autism will probably have expertise in functional behavioral analysis (FBA), which could be helpful in meeting the needs of students with consistent serious discipline problems who would benefit from an FBA. This teacher may be willing to complete FBAs with students not in her class if she is given additional support. A math teacher may have exceptional classroom management skills and can be a coach for other teachers. An art teacher might be willing to develop some art activities to integrate with the social skills instruction. A student club may be willing to create posters that can be used when teaching social skills or illustrating behavioral expectations. The planning team needs to recognize and use such talents and skills. Responsibilities for teaching and supervising can be reallocated to meet identified student needs and achieve desired outcomes.

Most talented, skilled individuals are already busy, but purposeful task delegation and responsibility adjustment can ensure that no one is overburdened. Evaluating priorities enables the most important tasks to be done first. One role of administrators is setting priorities, and when priorities are disputed, administrators use the problem-solving process (discussed in Chapters 6 and 9) to facilitate positive resolution of conflicts.

Physical Resources

Although adequate funding is important, in our experience money is usually not the deciding factor in successful model implementation. The most significant factor is the use of evidence-based practices that build capacity through ongoing professional development and coaching. Excellent administrators, coordinators, and coaches who provide meaningful teacher instruction over time are significant variables that strongly affect teacher buy-in, student participation, and parent support. Extra funds may be required to provide teacher training, to pay the presenters, to pay teachers for staying past their contracted time, or to buy reinforcers for students and teachers.

Gathering funds can be a time-consuming task that diverts energies away from creating services that will directly benefit students. The committee can start with building administrators who may have funds set aside for student services, such as assemblies, that could be diverted to help pay for supplies or professional development. Funds for character education or Title I funds may be a part of building budgets that could be used to support implementation efforts, especially teacher training.

Districts also may have some funds set aside for student services that could be accessed. SWPBS is focused on prevention and early intervention, and some special education funds are intended for this type of work. Safe and Drug-Free Schools grants may also provide some resources. Funds set aside by districts for new curricula or new materials could also be appropriated. Some states have small grants that usually have a simplified application process, and many professional organizations have mini grants. Federal grants tend to be quite difficult to obtain and are time consuming to write, although some grant applications are feasible for school districts to complete.

> **An important aspect of gathering funds is knowing the conditions that govern each funding source.**

An important aspect of gathering funds is knowing the conditions that govern each funding source. A one-time mini grant may help in getting started, but it will not sustain the process over time. If district administrators agree to allocate some funds from another budget item for a limited time to see whether the program really works, their commitment to long-term change may be limited. Initially, securing long-term sustainable funding that reflects building and district commitment is preferable.

Discussions with administrators (building, district, or state) regarding funds should consider these issues (Office of Special Education Programs, n.d.):

1. How does the funding (or lack of funding) align with priorities?
2. Is this funding opportunity a one-time event, or will this funding continue over time?
3. If funding is available over time, what documentation or accountability is needed to ensure its continuation?
4. How have similar initiatives been funded in the past?
5. How can funding be incorporated into current and future budgets?

CREATING BUY-IN
FROM TEACHERS AND OTHER SCHOOL STAKEHOLDERS

Establishing buy-in from teachers and other stakeholders is a task that requires a strong emphasis from the beginning; Figure 4.3 summarizes this process. Explaining SWPBS, the role of stakeholders, expected outcomes, and resources needed are some activities that create commitment to move forward. There are strategic ways to create buy-in. A self-assessment that asks two essential questions can be helpful:

1. What school-based data show that change is needed?
2. How can we build teacher consensus and teacher confidence in having or being able to get the skills needed for change?

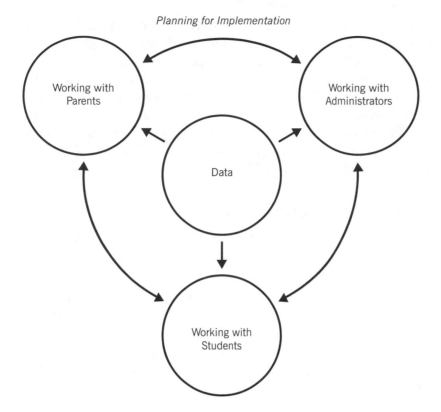

FIGURE 4.3. Using data to create buy-in.

Using Data

Completing a self-assessment generates data that can support this type of systems change. Such data may influence doubting teachers toward consensus, emphasizing what is actually happening at the school rather than what some perceive or believe to be problems or strengths. Often, perception data (e.g., a teacher says the school is "doing fine," or an administrator indicates that school suspensions are not excessive) is debatable; but hard data (e.g., number of in-school suspensions or instances of office referrals for disrespectful behavior) provide specific points of comparison and contrast. Used together, these data sources can provide evidence that change is needed.

Data also help to determine whether there is or can be sufficient consensus to support the proposed changes. Discerning faculty and staff consensus is a crucial first step. Generally, support from about 80% of school person-

> **Discerning faculty and staff consensus is a crucial first step.**

nel can be considered consensus. Explaining the underlying principles and ideas that support the change (i.e., behaviors are learned, behaviors can be changed by targeted teaching and reinforcement) are key committee functions. The committee must also help the school community understand the vision and connect with their own possible roles and challenges. Concerns or critical comments may represent valid problems that will inhibit the application of new ideas. Listening to and addressing these concerns are important. The committee will need to consider reasons for the lack of agreement and address those reasons as fully as possible.

George Batsche, an experienced advocate of RTI, points out that change is likely when two conditions exist: (1) "[Teachers] understand the need for the change," and (2) "they believe that they either possess the skills necessary to implement the change or have the support for acquiring the skills necessary to implement the change" (n.d.). Understanding the necessity of change comes with understanding the data and asking, "Are we happy with the data?" (Batsche). If the committee and school leaders are satisfied with the data and the outcomes, change may not be necessary and work should not be expended in creating change. The data should drive the efforts of the administration, the committee, the coordinator, and the teacher training program—everything that is done should be based on data.

Working with District Administrators

A continuum of services within a building is best established with school district support. Without this support, other initiatives from the state or district may consume the time, focus, and energy of the school. For example, the teaching approach to discipline utilized in this model requires professional development. If a new district writing curriculum also requires professional development, the district training will take precedence over the individual school training.

During initial phases, the school committee will benefit from having conversations with the district leaders to guide their planning and ensure that they are not working at odds with district plans. The following questions might guide the conversation (adapted from Sugai et al., 2010):

1. How does this model support district goals? How can the district leaders clear the way for implementation?
2. Does the district endorse the model, and will district administrators provide organizational and financial support and, as needed, flexibility?
3. What concerns do the district administrators express regarding the SWPBS model?
4. What problems might be created by changes in some aspects of the roles and responsibilities of teachers and administrators? For example, can a social skills class comprising mostly general education students be team taught for 1 hour per day by the school counselor and the special education teacher?
5. Will the amount and kind of professional development selected by the committee compete with district initiatives, thus impeding the building-level inservice?
6. Are district resources that could help in implementing the model available? Could district specialists provide some of the workshops? Can district funds or minigrants be allocated to the building?
7. How will the building committee be accountable to the district?

Several district administrators may need to be involved in conversations on these issues. Usually a district administrator of secondary education will be the primary contact for the building principal and thus should be informed of new initiatives. The administrator over curriculum is usually aware of professional development needs and can help coordinate inservice efforts. A representative from human resources can provide information about changing professional roles. Those involved with student support services (e.g., school counselors, school psychologists, social workers, and others) may have expertise to support training and other activities. If there is a district grant writer, he or she may know of funding opportunities. Working with a variety of district-level personnel can maximize collaboration and partnership.

Working with Parents and Community Members

Having parents thoroughly involved in the planning, implementation, and evaluation processes ensures the support of this important stakeholder group. If teachers and administrators move forward without the insights, support, and reflections of parents, they may find that they have to spend additional time updating parents, convincing them of the worthiness of the efforts, and then working to gain their support. Furthermore, parent perspectives can be valuable in

> **If teachers and administrators move forward without the insights, support, and reflections of parents, they may find that they have to spend additional time updating parents, convincing them of the worthiness of the efforts, and then working to gain their support.**

understanding the data, generating solutions, and gathering resources from the community. Ultimately school districts are accountable to their constituencies (i.e., parents) and involving parents in this process is one way of addressing the accountability issue.

The role of parents on the school committee includes helping the educators know what messages are important to parents. Generally, parents want to know the following (Jennings, n.d.):

- What is the general plan?
- How will it be implemented?
- How will students be selected to participate in levels of interventions?
- What specific information will be collected about their child, why is this information needed, and how will it be used?
- What will happen if students are not meeting expectations and what kind of help is available for these students?

Parents want to know what the school is doing and why; they want to be part of the process. Basic information can be provided in a number of ways beyond a blurb in a newsletter. Established groups, such as the Parent Student Teacher Association or the School Community Council, can provide information. Ideas may be passed on in conversations at parent–teacher conferences or back-to-school night, and e-mails and school websites can be utilized. Special activities or lessons can be included on the school calendar or on a highly visible bulletin board (Parent Engagement in Colorado School-wide PBS Schools, n.d.). Using a variety of means to communicate with parents is vital.

Parenting groups may also be included in the implementation plans. Parents want youth to be successful, and they want to work *with* school personnel to help their teen make good decisions and develop behaviors that lead to success. Teaching parents about the positive expectations and emphasizing their role in teaching and reinforcing these expectations are important. For example, if a school decides to use homeroom time to explicitly teach social skills (e.g., how to follow directions or how to respond to teasing), parents can be informed about the scheduling for the lessons, steps in using the skills, and ways they can help their student use those skills at home. Certainly, both of these skills would be useful at home.

Parents of students involved in Tier 2 and 3 interventions (see Chapters 8 and 9, respectively) should understand the nature of the intervention, the intended outcomes, and the importance of their role in supporting and facilitating change. For example, parents may need helping learning how to make an out-of-school suspension a teaching event rather than just punishment. Data collected about parental perceptions will help school committees involve parents in meaningful ways, partnering with them to teach youth positive behaviors and meet the emotional learning needs of students. Form 4.1 (at the end of this chapter) provides a sample parent survey.

Parents can provide information about the broader culture of the community; they may understand how events that are happening outside of school impact the school setting. Parents may be able to gather resources from community businesses to use for student rewards or as teacher appreciation tokens (adapted from Jennings, n.d.).

Working with Students

Including a few students on the planning team is essential in secondary schools. Students understand which positive reinforcement strategies will be meaningful to other students and can anticipate which plans are likely to create positive behavioral change. Students may help adult committee members understand the subtleties of the data that indicate problems are occurring, thus facilitating a strategically targeted response. Students may not need to attend every meeting, especially at the beginning of the implementation process, but the committee should frequently seek their perceptions, ideas, and involvement.

The students who participate in the planning team could function as a representative of a student organization that plans and carries out a variety of supportive activities. The authors have worked in schools where students have planned and presented school assemblies to teach and model the behavioral expectations and social skills being taught. Some student groups formed friendshipping activities, community service projects, parent and family nights, or other similar activities.

BUILDING CAPACITY THROUGH TEACHER DEVELOPMENT

To create a sustainable system for improving behavior in secondary schools, ongoing, relevant professional development for teachers must be provided; Figure 4.4 summarizes this aspect of planning for implementation. Teacher development is one facet of capacity building, an important aspect of sustainability. A recent analysis of teacher development research established some important guidelines for the sort of ongoing teacher training that will be most likely to meaningfully influence student behavior (Darling-Hammond, Wei, Andree, Richardson, & Orphanos, 2009). In this section we draw from and expound upon several of these guidelines.

Establishing Alignment

One of the most crucial aspects of successful teacher training is alignment between training and teacher goals. If teachers are to fully engage in training so that it impacts their own and their students' behavior, they must understand how the training (e.g., teaching social skills or

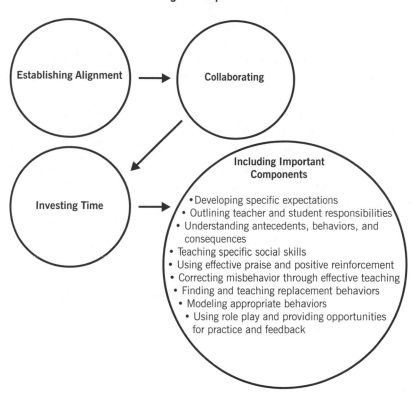

FIGURE 4.4. Building capacity through teacher development.

problem solving) will enhance their own goals and daily practice as teachers. Providing meaningful incentives for participation is vital. Linking school and teacher goals and practices to concrete student outcomes contributes to teachers' understanding about the purpose of the training. For

> One of the most crucial aspects of successful teacher training is alignment between training and teacher goals.

example, some teachers may feel that too much time is spent managing student behavior (e.g., Little, 2005), leaving insufficient time for academic instruction; others may be struggling with delivering quality academic instruction because of student misbehavior. Alignment may involve collecting data on time spent dealing with problem behaviors, setting goals to reduce that time through effective behavior interventions, and then following up with ongoing, meaningful feedback on improved practice and outcomes.

Providing well-aligned training requires thoughtful use of data. Rather than simply reporting the number of decreased ODRs, relevant data might show that the reduction of ODRs from 75 to 35 per month saved 600 minutes of instructional time (assuming that each ODR required about 15 minutes of office time to resolve). With the meaningful goal of increasing time for instruction, administration, collaboration, and so on, teachers can readily understand the relevance of training that reduces their time spent in managing student misbehavior. These benefits require that ongoing information be provided on how their efforts are closing the gap toward goals they support.

Collaborating

Collaboration between teachers and other stakeholders is vital; it facilitates the generalization of teaching training that creates noticeable schoolwide improvement. Relevant data showing such improvement becomes part of the impetus for teachers to continue their efforts. Collaboration can be encouraged through a variety of strategies (Darling-Hammond et al., 2009).

First, teachers can be encouraged (with time and incentives) to observe and provide feedback for each other as they implement practices derived from training—benefiting both the observed and the observer. Research has linked this sort of observation and feedback to more student-centered and mastery-focused instruction, which goes beyond simply relaying content. Teachers have also reported increased learning opportunities through such collaboration along with an increased desire to continue learning (Darling-Hammond et al., 2009).

Having teachers record their teaching and then share teaching vignettes with colleagues can also encourage collaboration and engagement with training material. Teachers could consider how they used effective discipline or how they taught positive routines. This approach has also been associated with improved teaching practices (Darling-Hammond et al., 2009). Another practice that strengthens teacher collaboration is the creating of consistent blocks of time for teachers to meet, plan, and discuss progress with each other, parents, and other stakeholders.

Investing Time

A recent survey regarding SWPBS found that teacher buy-in is often relatively low in secondary schools (Flannery, Sugai, & Anderson, 2009). These survey authors reported that "Survey results suggested that just 50% of school staff were generally supportive of adopting a SWPBS approach; however, actual active participation was noticeably lower" (p. 184). In order to obtain teacher support and improve participation, teachers need to be convinced that their efforts will be worthwhile. Interestingly, it seems that as the time invested in a given approach increases, teachers may become more likely to support and participate effectively in school improvement efforts (Darling-Hammond et al., 2009). Conversely, failure to invest sufficient time in teacher training may send the message that the program is unimportant and not worth the effort—resulting in a downward spiral in participation.

According to research, teacher training that leads to improvements in student outcomes requires a significant time investment. Training of fewer than 15 total hours did not result in significant improvement in student outcomes, whereas training sequences that averaged 49 total hours (ranging from 30 to 100) did show a measurable impact (Darling-Hammond et al., 2009). The 49-hour training may involve not only instruction but also in-class observations, feedback, collaboration, and data sharing; training teachers is really about establishing a culture. Professional development represents a fairly intensive time and resource commitment, which requires understanding that the return (in time, compensation, improved teaching, student improvement, etc.) will be worth the investment.

However, not all of this time investment requires training outside of the classroom. Occasional, sporadic training workshops are not effective (Darling-Hammond et al., 2009), but if training is also brought into the classroom, integrated into focus groups, followed with collaborative in-class observations and feedback, tied to relevant and regular data sharing, blogged about, discussed in the break room—in short, if the training becomes a part of the school culture—49 hours can be reasonably surpassed, practices can change, and student outcomes should improve.

Teachers also see the link between time investment and effectiveness. According to a national survey, "Sustained and intensive professional development is more likely to have an impact, as reported by teachers, than is shorter professional development" (Garet, Porter, Desimone, Birman, & Yoon, 2001, p. 935). Since teachers understand this link between time and effectiveness, more time spent in teacher development—tied specifically to improving behavior in the schools—will likely increase teacher confidence (and thus perhaps buy-in) as well as effectiveness.

Including Important Components

The specifics of training should ultimately be tied to goals at each intervention level or tier, and readers can draw from subsequent chapters (particularly Chapters 5, 8, and 9) for information that will need to be communicated to teachers as part of training. The following list suggests specific topics that can be considered particularly important for teacher training:

- Developing and expressing clear and specific expectations.
- Outlining teacher and student responsibilities.
- Understanding antecedents, behaviors, and consequences.
- Teaching specific social skills.
- Using effective praise and positive reinforcement.
- Correcting misbehavior through effective teaching.
- Finding and teaching replacement behaviors.
- Modeling appropriate behaviors.
- Using role play and providing opportunities for practice and feedback.

Other topics targeted to achieve specific outcomes could be identified and included in this list through considering data from teacher and parents surveys. Various forms of outcome data could include disciplinary records (e.g., the number and types of student suspensions or ODRs).

SUMMARY

To begin developing a comprehensive system for addressing behavioral needs, school leadership begins by organizing a committee to initiate these efforts. Representatives should be included from relevant stakeholder groups (e.g., teachers, administrators, parents, students), and their roles and responsibilities should be clearly outlined. This committee should assess the needs of the school along with available resources on the school and district levels. With these preliminary tasks accomplished, a significant level of support should be obtained, and specific training and implementation can begin. The next chapters discuss needs and issues specific to each level or tier involved with implementing a comprehensive system for improving behavior in secondary schools.

Parent Survey

	Strongly agree	Agree	Neutral	Disagree	Strongly disagree
My child's school is a safe and positive school.					
The teachers at my child's school care about my child.					
I know what behavior is expected from my child at school.					
I am satisfied with the behavior expectations at my child's school.					
I am familiar with schoolwide positive behavior support (SWPBS) at my child's school.					
My child's school teaches respect and responsibility to students.					
My child's school has a bullying problem.					
My child's teachers provide appropriate emotional support for students when needed.					
My child's school communicates well with parents.					

Comments

What student behaviors do you think are the biggest problem at our school?

How could our school help your child experience success at school?

What else do school leaders need to know to help meet the social, emotional, or behavioral needs of your child?

CHAPTER 5

Schoolwide Interventions
Tier 1

Jackie was beginning her second year as principal at Jefferson Middle School. She was dreading the opening of school because of the constant influx of office disciplinary referrals (ODRs)—over 700 the previous year. Jackie and her colleagues felt like they were spending all of their time dealing with discipline and neglecting academics. She wondered whether there was something she could do to improve this negative situation at her school.

She contacted the district behavior specialist, Doug, for assistance. During their first meeting they examined all of the ODR data, looking for patterns (where problems were occurring, which students were involved, etc.) and discussing options for resolving the problem. The data showed that more than 200 of the school's 450 students had been referred to the office for discipline at least once. Of those 200, about 15 had more than 10 ODRs, and an additional 50 students had between 2 and 9. They learned that 65% of the ODRs resulted from incidents in the classroom, with the remaining 35% occurring in nonclassroom environments (e.g., school grounds, lunchroom, and hallways). They also learned that more than 50% took place when less-structured activities were more common. In reviewing the typical consequences for ODRs, they discovered that over 90% were punitive in some way (e.g., in-school suspension, suspension). It was obvious from these data that this was a schoolwide problem, not just the misbehavior of a few students—although a few students did create a lot of problems. Jackie and Doug also decided that the solution had to be a schoolwide team approach, relying more on positive, proactive strategies.

Jackie's experience is not unusual. As discussed in Chapter 2, many have noted that transitioning from elementary to secondary schools involves many challenges: larger school and class sizes; more impersonal, bureaucratic administrative procedures; and nonindividualized, departmentalized instruction (Eccles, Lord, & Midgely, 1991). Secondary students can lose interest in and motivation for school, often resulting in lower academic achievement. Truancy and other problem behaviors can also increase in secondary schools. These conditions may compound risk factors for adolescents who are already academically, socially, or emotionally vulnerable. This chapter discusses what can be done to help address such concerns schoolwide as part of Tier 1 or universal-level SWPBS intervention.

THE IMPORTANCE OF EXPECTATIONS

Creating and teaching expectations for positive behaviors is a fundamental feature of several well-known schoolwide approaches to behavior, such as SWPBS, social and emotional learning, and schoolwide discipline plans. Effective schools establish from the beginning of the school year how students are expected to behave, and throughout the year teachers discuss expectations and boundaries with students.

> **Students who are striving to meet high behavioral expectations are less likely to exhibit inappropriate behaviors.**

High expectations are important for several reasons. First, students who are striving to meet high behavioral expectations are less likely to exhibit inappropriate behaviors. Second, expectations let everyone know exactly what behavior is desired. For example, most youth try to please the important adults in their lives, those with whom they have a relationship based on mutual respect and trust. Often administrators and teachers assume that students will just intuitively know what is wanted without having to be told or directly taught. Sometimes students will know that what they are doing will not please adults, but if they have not been taught another way to meet a particular need, they often resort to inappropriate behaviors because they lack alternatives. Other times students choose inappropriate behaviors because experience has shown them that such behaviors can help them get attention, obtain something that they want, and/or avoid things they dislike that are uncomfortable or painful. Third, teachers with high expectations communicate to students that they are capable of achieving meaningful outcomes. Knowing that someone else believes in them may be crucial in helping some students stay engaged when challenges arise and they feel discouraged. While it is important to adopt and communicate high expectations, it is also important to ensure that those expectations are reasonable and achievable; otherwise students can become frustrated.

Consistency in implementing expectations is also important. When expectations are reasonable and achievable, school personnel find it easier to be consistent in following through with program implementation. As expressed by Young et al. (2008),

> **If we relent and tolerate low expectations, we are in effect demonstrating to the student that less is acceptable.**

If we relent and tolerate low expectations, we are in effect demonstrating to the student that less is acceptable. The student may see us as inconsistent and perhaps unfair. He learns that we can be manipulated. If the student meets expectations, be certain to reinforce them. If the student continues to struggle, re-teach the expected behavior rather than punish. What you do as the teacher impacts the student's behavior immensely. If the student is making a sincere effort and is unable to meet the expectation, you may need to divide the expected task/behavior into smaller steps. Nonetheless, the final goal should remain the same, and you should keep teaching, encouraging, and believing in the student until that goal is reached. (p. 21)

Returning to the example of Jefferson Middle School, after Jackie's initial meeting with Doug, she worked with the current school discipline committee to transform that group to a team that would develop a new, positive approach to discipline. At Doug's suggestion, the school adopted SWPBS. The new team became the school's SWPBS team. One of the team's first tasks was the development of clear positive expectations for student behavior.

Creating Behavioral Expectations in Secondary Schools

Creating clear behavioral expectations in secondary schools may be more challenging than in elementary schools. Just under half of high school teachers involved in one study supported implementing key behavioral strategies of acknowledging and positively reinforcing appropriate student behavior (Flannery et al., 2009). Another difference between secondary and elementary schools is the greater degree of secondary student involvement in SWPBS as discussed in Chapter 4. Because secondary students are capable of active involvement in school activities, they should be involved in the planning and implementation of schoolwide expectations. The success of SWPBS depends on understanding secondary students' perspectives regarding expectations and the subtleties of data collected by school teams. Fenning (2004) provides an example of how a high school utilized students in producing a video demonstrating the schoolwide expectations. The students participated in personal interviews and mock scenes illustrating students following school expectations; the final video was shown at a schoolwide assembly.

Secondary schools appear to emphasize broad expectations that can be defined differently in different settings. For example, Flannery et al. (2009) found that most high schools reported emphasizing *respect* and *responsibility*, and many included *learning* expectations (e.g., perseverance, achievement). Such broad expectations are best expressed in terms of more specific behaviors as shown in the examples below:

- *Respect for self.* Keep dress and grooming appropriate for school.
- *Respect for others.* Use polite expressions and greetings with others.
- *Respect for property.* Leave public areas in the school neat and clean.

An essential part of establishing clear expectations is posting rules as reminders for both teachers and students. In secondary schools one might want to discuss with teachers and students using the word *expectations* instead of *rules*. We would encourage the use of the word *expectations* because it may diminish the potentially coercive tone of the word *rules*—this helps recognize the desire for increasing autonomy of secondary students. Teachers can emphasize the expectations when they are teaching positive behavior or correcting misbehavior. Teachers must also reinforce students when they meet expectations and follow rules. The combination of teaching and reinforcing positive behavior is the most powerful way of helping students learn to behave within the boundaries established by the faculty. Faculty can help students become confident in what they are expected to do (or not do) by posting, reviewing, and reinforcing schoolwide expectations. Posting provides a visual reminder of the expectations for students and a prompt for additional instruction by the teacher (e.g., see Figure 5.1) (Black & Downs, 1993, p. 43). When specific rules are given, *examples* and *nonexamples* can be provided, demonstrating what each rule looks like in various school contexts. Examples make rules and expectations very clear, ensuring that students know exactly what behaviors are expected (Taylor-Greene et al., 1997). Several additional guidelines are noted by Young et al. (2008, p. 24) that can help make this process more effective:

> **The combination of teaching and reinforcing positive behavior is the most powerful way of helping students learn to behave within the boundaries established by the faculty.**

> **Posting provides a visual reminder of the expectations for students and a prompt for additional instruction by the teacher.**

How to Accept "No" for an Answer

1. Look at the person.

2. Say "OK."

3. No arguing, whining, or pouting.

4. If you don't understand why, ask calmly for a reason.

5. If you disagree or have a complaint, make arrangements to talk about it later.

FIGURE 5.1. Sample poster of a schoolwide expectation.

- Limit the number of rules or expectations to *no more than three to five*. The goal is to promote student success. Expectations must be high, but reasonable.
- *State rules positively.* For example, "Keep your hands and feet to yourself" is better than "No hitting, pushing, or kicking." Give students something they can do that can be reinforced.
- Include *positive consequences* for following the expectations. Group contingencies work well. For example, a special class activity could be scheduled if everyone comes to class prepared for 5 days.
- Include mild *negative consequences* for not following the expectations, when necessary. However, remember that the best form of discipline is teaching, not punishing.
- Use *natural consequences* wherever possible. Natural consequences are a logical result of the student's action. For example, a natural consequence of not bringing a pencil to class would be to use one of the old broken "stubbies" from the collection of homeless pencils. Avoid using consequences that interfere with learning or that might actually be reinforcing to the student: for example, do not send the student to his or her locker to get a pencil.
- Be sure the expectation is *observable and measurable*. If a behavior cannot be seen or counted, it should not be used as a rule. For example, "Raise your hand to be called on in class" is observable and measurable, whereas "Respect others" is not because it does not specify the expected behaviors.

A good example of the use of schoolwide expectations to improve student behavior in a middle school is discussed in Metzler, Biglan, Rusby, and Sprague (2001). Doug, the behavior specialist in the opening vignette, recommended to Jackie that the school faculty read the Metzler et al. article, which describes how a school staff clarified rules, taught and positively reinforced expected social behaviors, provided mild consequences for rule violations, and monitored data on students' behavior. Schoolwide expectations were also formed into four school rules:

1. Be respectful.
2. Put-ups not put-downs.

3. Cooperate with others.
4. Solve problems peacefully.

For each rule, specific desired behaviors were identified, and 50-minute lesson plans about these expectations were developed and taught by teachers. Results included a decrease in students' aggressive behaviors and improvement in perceptions of school safety. The Jefferson Middle School adopted an approach similar to that of the Metzler et al. study, but they added a schoolwide social skills component.

TEACHING SOCIAL SKILLS TO ALL STUDENTS

After establishing rules and expectations for appropriate behaviors, it is helpful for teachers to proactively teach social skills in the classroom. Teaching social skills is integral to SWPBS. Some students have had few opportunities to learn and practice specific social skills. The common assumption that students know how to behave in school may be inaccurate. It may be safer to assume that students need instruction regarding appropriate social behavior; a way to provide this instruction is through schoolwide teaching of social skills. To develop and implement a schoolwide social skills curriculum, we need (1) to understand the nature of social skills, (2) to identify and define the specific social skills appropriate for students and relevant to the needs of the school, (3) to assess students' social skills, and (4) to teach the social skills and encourage their use.

> After establishing rules and expectations for appropriate behaviors, it is helpful for teachers to proactively teach social skills in the classroom.

The Nature of Social Skills

Social skills are those behaviors that are necessary for students to successfully interact with others. Examining the characteristics of youth or adults who are socially skilled reveals three fundamental aspects of their behavior. First, the word *social* refers to interpersonal interactions between two or more individuals. Thus behavior such as having a conversation with another person, making a polite request, or asking someone to join an activity are all social skills.

Second, skills require action. A social skill must be a positive action, such as engaging in conflict resolution. Simply not fighting is not engaging a social skill. In this case, if a replacement behavior for fighting is identified, such as positive problem solving, we now have an appropriate social skill to teach. In designing a social skills program for an individual or an entire school, the planning team must focus on the skills they would like the students to acquire, not the problem behavior they want to eliminate.

Third, to be considered socially competent a student must be capable not only of using the social skills but of using the skills in appropriate contexts (e.g., with the right people, at the right time, and in the right place). A socially skilled person performs appropriate social behaviors repeatedly and consistently. For example, a socially skilled student knows not only how to be assertive, but also when and with whom. A skilled person has the ability to perform a behavior well under a variety of circumstances. The actions of socially skilled individuals are natural, genuine, and comfortable. Thus becoming socially skilled requires time, practice, coaching, and reinforcement.

Social skills are behaviors valued by others; they are important and worthwhile interactions, but they may vary from one culture or subculture to another. The society and the cultural groups within that society define what behaviors constitute social competence within their community. In school students are expected to follow directions and comply with authority figures; students who act accordingly are usually considered socially skilled, at least by school personnel. Assessing the student's cultural environment to determine what behaviors are considered socially acceptable is important. Students may need to be acculturated through more direct teaching, practice, and reinforcement if their culture does not support the use of such skills.

> **In summary, social skills are interactions between two or more persons; the skills involve action; and the interactions are positive, effective, and valued by society.**

In summary, social skills are interactions between two or more persons; the skills involve action; and the interactions are positive, effective, and valued by society. Socially skilled persons consistently display these interpersonal behaviors at the appropriate times, in appropriate situations, and in a natural manner. Researchers have documented that students with social skills deficits have both short- and long-term problems, including school failure, school dropout, social rejection, interpersonal conflicts, unemployment and job instability, mental health problems, and economic challenges (see Merrell & Gimpel, 1998, and Merrell & Gueldner, 2010).

Social Skills Assessments

Assessments should be conducted to determine the students' social skills strengths and deficits. Effective assessment strategies include checklists, role playing, and direct observation, among other procedures. A detailed description of social skills assessment is beyond the scope of this chapter. An excellent source of information regarding social skills assessment can be found in Merrell and Gimpel's (1998) book *Social Skills of Children and Adolescents*.

Other useful schoolwide assessments to aid in selection of social skills to teach include interviews, observations, focus groups, archival data, systematic screening for behavior disorders, and data from office discipline referrals (Marchant et al., 2009). For example, reviewing ODR data may reveal that a significant number of students are sent to the office for failing to follow teacher directions. Teaching students how to follow instructions could be a reasonable next step.

Another resource to help in the selection of specific social skills to teach is to use social skill taxonomies, classification systems that are frequently used to categorize behaviors. Caldarella and Merrell (1997) developed such a system by reviewing 21 research investigations involving the assessment of social skills and indentified five frequently occurring social skill dimensions: peer relationships, self-management, academic, compliance, and assertion. They also provide examples of specific social skills under each of these dimensions that school teams could focus on.

Based on the chosen assessment method, identifying and prioritizing the specific social skills to be taught and the steps for teaching each skill become primary tasks of the team. Social skills lessons should be taught based on student needs, usually every week or two so that the ideas remain fresh in students' and teachers' minds (see Goldstein, 1999, and Kerr & Nelson, 2006, pp. 239–245, for good examples of social skills lessons).

The SWPBS team at Jefferson Middle School requested participation of all teachers in the school in selecting five critical social skills to be taught to all students. They used a four-step process: (1) the SWPBS team reviewed ODR data to determine which discipline problems might have been avoided by use of specific socials skills; (2) all teachers were asked to use the social skills checklist provided in *Skillstreaming the Adolescent* (Goldstein, McGinnis, Sprafkin, Gershaw, & Klein, 1997) to identify the five social skills they thought most important for their school; (3) the SWPBS team combined the skills identified in steps 1 and 2 and narrowed the list to the five most needed skills for their school; and (4) the SWPBS team met with all faculty, discussed the list, made minor modifications, and finalized the following five social skills they all agreed to teach:

1. How to follow directions.
2. How to give and accept compliments.
3. How to solve problems with others.
4. How to offer help or assistance to others.
5. How to express appreciation to others.

After agreeing to focus on these five social skills, the SWPBS team next needed to address how to train their staff to teach these skills in a way that students would learn how to use them.

Teaching Social Skills

Particular methods and procedures have been found to be effective in teaching social skills to children and youth. Walker et al. (2004, p. 208) identify some guidelines of social skills training, which include the following:

- Social skills are best taught in naturalistic settings and situations such as classrooms, though they can also be taught in small groups or counseling situations.
- Social skills should be taught by the same procedures and principles used to teach academic skills, including direct instruction, modeling, practice opportunities, feedback, and reinforcement when skills are successfully displayed.
- A direct, positive relationship should be evident between the extent and quality of social skills training and changes in social behavior.
- Social skills training should be supplemented by behavioral rehearsal opportunities or practice, performance feedback, and contingency systems in naturalistic settings to promote use, fluency, and mastery of the skills taught in more formal instructional settings.

The way social skills are taught to students can be as important as the skills themselves. The next section presents the rationale for teaching social skills and presents the instructional procedures that are most effective in helping students become socially competent. Much of

> **The way social skills are taught to students can be as important as the skills themselves.**

this material is based on the work of Young and colleagues (see Young et al., 2008) who have spent many years training educators in social skills instruction.

Social Skills Rationales

> **By explaining why we want students to engage in the appropriate behavior, we demonstrate that there is logic behind our request, teaching students that outcomes for their behaviors are predictable rather than haphazard.**

A rationale is a reason or justification given to students for learning and using specific social skills. By explaining why we want students to engage in the appropriate behavior, we demonstrate that there is logic behind our request, teaching students that outcomes for their behaviors are predictable rather than haphazard. A rationale for teaching students how to accept feedback or criticism is illustrated in the following statement from a member of school staff:

"When teachers correct your behavior, you must look at them and listen to what they have to say without arguing. Accepting feedback helps you understand how your behavior is seen by others and allows you to learn from them; it also shows respect, and helps you build positive relationships. By showing respect, you are less likely to be sent to the principal's office for discipline."

> **The most effective rationales have certain common characteristics: they are brief, believable, and personal to the student.**

The most effective rationales have certain common characteristics: they are brief, believable, and personal to the student. When a student asks why something is important, many adults respond by saying "Because I said so." A more helpful and instructive way to respond is to use one of the following three types of rationales:

1. Explain the *benefits* of using appropriate behavior or avoiding inappropriate behavior: for example, others trust us when we behave in a polite and civil manner.
2. Remind the student of possible negative consequences or punishments that may follow misbehavior. Teach students that using positive social skills will help them *avoid unpleasant consequences*.
3. Teach students that appropriate social behavior *shows others that we care* about their needs as well as our own.

Instructional Procedures

Adults are sometimes reluctant to teach social skills to youth because of concerns that the process is overly complex or requires specialized training. However, the instructional procedures to teach such skills are fairly easy, though they may require some practice to become natural to the teacher. The following simple process is often used to teach a social skill to a group of students or to an individual:

1. Begin by telling the students what specific social skill they are going to learn and describe each step included in the skill. Have students repeat out loud the steps of the skill.

2. Explain to the students the rationale or reasons why it is important to learn and use this skill.

3. Demonstrate the social skill for the students. For some skills you may want to demonstrate both using and failing to use the skill: for example, demonstrating how to make a polite request versus demanding something. This process helps students more clearly discriminate when their behavior is socially correct.

4. Have students practice the skill several times. Just as academic behaviors require many opportunities to practice, so do social behaviors.

> **Just as academic behaviors require many opportunities to practice, so do social behaviors.**

5. Provide specific feedback on each step of the social skill as students practice: praising appropriate social behavior, correcting mistakes, and reinforcing students' attempts to use the skill correctly.

6. Provide opportunities for students to practice the social skills in natural settings to ensure that behavior is maintained over time and the skill use is generalized to multiple settings. Giving the students specific assignments to practice outside of the instructional setting helps to promote natural use of the skill.

Below is an example of how teachers at Jefferson Middle School used the teaching process with the specific social skill of giving a compliment. They used a dialogue like the following for each of the steps of the skill, and posted the social skill steps as a visual prompt to students and teachers:

1. Name the social skill and describe the steps for performing the skill. "Today I am going to teach you how to give someone a compliment. The steps are:

   a. Decide on a behavior that deserves a compliment,

   b. Look at the person,

   c. Use a pleasant voice, and

   d. Say the praise statement."

   The teacher might give this example and review: "Steve, I thought you made a great comment in class today recognizing Angela's presentation on Shakespeare. You used the steps I am describing. Let's repeat the steps for the social skill of giving a compliment." After the class has repeated the steps in order, the teacher might praise them by saying, "You did a great job of repeating all four steps in order."

2. Give a rationale for why the skill is important. "It is important to give people compliments because our feedback helps them feel good about their behavior. Compliments also let people know that you like them and notice the good things they do. If we don't give positive feedback, people may feel uncomfortable and stop doing those good things. So our compliments strengthen the good behavior of others."

3. Demonstrate the social skill for the students.

   a. "I'm going to pretend that Simona has recently moved here and joined our class. She has smiled and been friendly to others. I will give her a compliment using the four steps."
   b. "I first look at her and then say in a pleasant voice, 'Simona, I like your smile. You seem friendly: Would you like to join us for lunch?'"

4. Have students practice the skill several times.

   a. Have the whole class say the steps in unison (choral responding).
   b. Have students says the steps individually, either to the class or (if the group is large) to a peer.
   c. Call on a student to role-play: "Pretend that I am a student who has recently joined your class. Show how you might give me a compliment."
   d. Have additional students role-play for the rest of the class.
   e. Have the students pair up and practice with each other. Monitor them so that you can give feedback and extra help when needed. Repeatedly reviewing the steps helps to establish fluent use of the skill in natural settings.

5. Provide feedback and praise on each step of the social skill.

   a. "You have remembered and said each step in the social skill of giving a compliment."
   b. "As I listened to you practice I noticed that each of you identified something positive about your partner. You also looked at each other and used a pleasant voice as you gave your compliment."

6. Have students practice these social skills in natural settings. "Now you all know how to give a compliment. I'll watch you this week. I want to see each of you give compliments the way we have practiced. If you can't remember all of the steps, check the poster on the bulletin board or ask me for help. The more you practice, the easier it will become."

The sample lesson above is scripted to guide teachers in learning the steps to teaching social skills. Our experience is that initially mastering scripted lessons helps instructors transition to teaching the skills in their own words without omitting any of the critical components. Addressing each instructional component of the lesson is critical if students are to master the social skills. For example, omitting practice will reduce students' ability to recall and implement the skills. But with practice, skill acquisition will become natural and more comfortable for both instructors and students.

Administrators and teachers at secondary schools have been successful in teaching selected social skills as part of SWPBS. When all students learn to use these basic social skills, an atmosphere of civility becomes the school norm. One way to accomplish this is to have all teachers spend 10 to 15 minutes three times per week teaching social skills in homeroom classes. However, instruction alone is not sufficient. All school personnel should

When all students learn to use these basic social skills, an atmosphere of civility becomes the school norm.

encourage and praise these social skills throughout school settings and across all classes and activities to achieve maintenance and generalization.

All school personnel should encourage and praise these social skills throughout school settings and across all classes and activities to achieve maintenance and generalization.

SCHOOLWIDE ENCOURAGEMENT AND PRAISE

Encouragement and praise are critical to all aspects of a student's life, not just learning and using social skills. School personnel must encourage academic performance along with socially appropriate behavior. It is common for students to experience doubt and uncertainty as they are trying to learn and use new skills. As their social environment becomes more challenging, many secondary school students find it difficult knowing how to interact appropriately. Encouragement can help students face issues that they may struggle with—things that are important but uncertain to them. Students must understand that it is all right to try and to sometimes fail because they can always try again. Encouragement acknowledges what is good in students, supports their efforts, and communicates that they can succeed. Sincere encouragement can foster feelings of courage and fortitude for facing their fears as well as building teacher–student relationships of trust.

As their social environment becomes more challenging, many secondary school students find it difficult knowing how to interact appropriately.

However, encouragement is used too infrequently in schools. Ironically, the students who need encouragement the most are often the least likely to receive it: "Children who misbehave are most likely to receive the least amount of encouragement . . . instead of building them up, we tear them down; instead of recognizing their efforts and improvements, we point out their mistakes" (Evans, 1997, p. 12). So it is important that all students, including those who do not know or use social skills, receive encouraging remarks from teachers. The following are examples of encouraging statements that could be used with secondary students:

Encouragement is used too infrequently in schools. Ironically, the students who need encouragement the most are often the least likely to receive it.

- "You can do this."
- "I can tell you worked hard on that assignment."
- "Remember, you've done things like this before."
- "I can see that you're not sure of yourself, but I believe in you."
- "Relax, you'll do better each time you try."

To make encouragement believable, such statements should be accompanied by specific reasons that are meaningful to the student and that the teacher believes he or she can succeed. These can be tied to the nature of the work, to the student's ability, or to both. For example, "Remember the last difficult assignment you completed by working hard and getting help from a friend. You can do this." This encouragement will more likely be perceived positively when the teacher and student have a positive, trusting relationship, which is critical in working with adolescents.

Praise also can be used to encourage students' efforts toward positive behavior. Praise is widely known to be effective in teaching and reinforcing appropriate behavior. Praising specific student behaviors was noted in Chapter 3 as a way for teachers to improve the classroom climate; praise is also an important part of SWPBS Tier 1 interventions. Teachers and administrators need to acknowledge and praise students' cooperation and attempts to do what is asked. While students' efforts may not be effective the first time or even the sixth time, it is important to let them know that their efforts are noticed and appreciated so that they continue to display appropriate behaviors.

Praise is a natural, nonintrusive intervention that can be used in schools (Sutherland, Wehby, & Copeland, 2000), considered to be perhaps the easiest classroom modification the general education teacher can make to address students' problem behaviors (Niesyn, 2009). Unfortunately, praise is used too infrequently and often lacks enough specificity to be effective. The use of specific praise in schools occurs at even lower rates. Students experiencing emotional or behavioral difficulties often receive little if any praise from adults.

To be effective, praise must include a statement that is contingent, specific, and immediate, and have a positive effect on student behavior (Marchant & Young, 2001). Teachers can reduce the frequency of problem behavior by using effective praise, thus saving time and energy previously spent responding to classroom disruptions. Teachers should find something for which to praise every student at least once per day, using praise consistently and contingently as a positive reinforcement strategy for increasing desired behaviors and reducing disruptive off-task behaviors. Satisfied students tend to receive more teacher praise and less negative teacher feedback than do dissatisfied students (Burnett, 2002). Praise has also been shown to help socially withdrawn and isolated students become more outgoing (Nelson, Caldarella, Young, & Webb, 2008; Moroz & Jones, 2002). Increasing effective praise and teaching corrective behaviors can positively influence those students who are repeatedly being sent to the principal's office for discipline.

Praise has been shown to be an essential component of SWPBS in middle schools. Nelson, Young, Young, and Cox (2010) examined the use of schoolwide teacher-to-student praise notes as part of SWPBS in a secondary school. Teachers were trained to use direct instruction in teaching social skills during their first-period classes and to write praise notes when students displayed these skills. Praise notes were given to students by their teachers, with a copy for parents. Teachers were reinforced with gift certificates to local restaurants when they reached benchmark numbers of praise notes written (e.g., 25, 60, 100, 150). Results revealed a significant negative correlation: as the number of praise notes increased, the number of student ODRs decreased considerably, saving student, teacher, and administrator time. Form 5.1 (at the end of the chapter) presents an example of a praise note that can be used in schools.

> **Increasing effective praise and teaching corrective behaviors can positively influence those students who are repeatedly being sent to the principal's office for discipline.**

Praise must be instructive—teaching students what behavior was noticed and why what they did was valued. For example, a general praise statement such as "Good job" is less instructive than "Susan, you followed all of the instructions on how to organize this paper, precisely as I directed. This helped you earn a higher grade on the assignment and also made it easier for me to understand your ideas. Nice job!" Students gain confidence when they know specifically what was positive in their behavior and why it was valued and important to others. The following steps help make praise instructive as well as reinforcing (see West et al., 1995):

1. Specifically state the behavior you are complimenting.
2. Provide a detailed description of what occurred.
3. Give a reason why the behavior was praiseworthy.
4. Provide a pleasant consequence.

These steps are provided to highlight the important elements of instructive praise but they should not be taken to imply that the note or the process needs to be long. Such a praise statement can be a valuable teaching moment accomplished in only 10 to 15 seconds. For example, all of these elements are found in the following statement: "I appreciate how well you listened while I gave instructions. I noticed you looked me in the eyes while I was talking. I am sure as a result you understand the assignment better, and in the future I will listen very carefully to your questions." West et al. (1995) show how the use of instructive praise as part of classroom teaching procedures helped improve the classroom behavior of middle school students. This study was conducted in several regular junior high classes of approximately 30 students in each class. Instructive praise could be used by every teacher as part of schoolwide Tier 1 interventions.

SCHOOLWIDE TOKEN ECONOMY SYSTEMS

Closely related to schoolwide praise is the use of schoolwide token economy, a common strategy used with behavior management. When using token economies teachers award "tokens" to reinforce students when they meet positive behavioral goals. Tokens are created by the school, often in the form of tickets or points that students earn by displaying desirable behaviors. Students may then exchange the points for reinforcing items or activities. A menu is typically created listing how many points are required to access particular reinforcers. These reinforcers do not need to be expensive—in fact, secondary students often find access to special privileges (e.g., having a few minutes of free time with peers, being able to make the school's morning announcements, listening to music during individual study time, being first in the lunch line) quite reinforcing, and they cost the school no additional money.

> **Token economy systems have been effective at improving student behavior in a variety of settings including special education, general education, and even college classrooms.**

Token economy systems have been effective at improving student behavior in a variety of settings including special education, general education, and even college classrooms. Token economies can also be used schoolwide as a universal-level SWPBS intervention (Sailor, Bradley, & Sims, 2009). Some important areas to address when designing token economy systems for use in schools include the following (see, e.g., Myles, Moran, Ormsbee, & Downing, 1992):

1. *Identifying target behaviors.* Target behaviors should be defined in measureable terms and be based on positive student behavioral outcomes (e.g., turning in class assignments on time, following teachers' instructions, and getting a teacher's attention appropriately).

2. *Specifying reinforcers.* Reinforcers should be purposefully chosen:
   - Student input should be included.
   - Reinforcers should be age appropriate such as a ticket with the student's name being submitted for a weekly schoolwide drawing for movie passes.
   - A variety of items and activities should be included as reinforcers.
   - Reinforcers should be accompanied by praise.
   - Eventually, reinforcers should be faded to naturally occurring social or academic reinforcers (e.g., permission to sit with chosen peers at an assembly).
3. *Planning token distribution and redemption strategies.* The school team should develop a system that can apply to all personnel and all students, and all need to understand it. The team should consider such issues as the following:
   - The schoolwide system needs to be relatively simple and not require a lot of time for the exchange of tokens.
   - Behavioral expectations and the rules for earning and receiving points should be taught to all students and publically posted in the building.
   - Decisions need to be made regarding the potential loss of points for inappropriate behavior. Taking points away tends to be viewed negatively by students and may create an unfortunate power struggle if a student feels the loss of points was unjustified. We recommend avoiding this.
   - It is important to establish a record-keeping plan that includes a record of points earned that is visible and accessible to students.

Let's return to the Jefferson Middle School SWPBS team for an example of a simple schoolwide token economy system. After agreeing on the five social skills that would be taught to all students, the team designed a reinforcement system to strengthen the use of the skills. A simple praise note that was developed for use as a token included five items: (1) a place for the student's name, (2) the date, (3) check boxes for the five social skills, (4) a comments section, and (5) a line for the teacher's signature. Copies of the notes were printed on (no carbon required) paper. A teacher who observed a student using any of the five social skills filled out a praise note and gave one copy to the student (who was encouraged to share it with his or her parents), providing positive feedback for use of the skill, and one copy to the office to serve as a token for a possible secondary reward. Every Friday, 10 notes were drawn from a box, names were read over the intercom, and the students were invited to come to the office after school to select a reward (e.g., a pencil, candy, movie pass, or positive note from the principal to the parents).

ADMINISTRATIVE INTERVENTIONS

Despite teachers' best attempts to teach and reinforce appropriate behaviors, sometimes students will violate schoolwide rules and expectations. When this occurs, administrative interventions may be a good approach (Black & Downs, 1993). Rather than being simply a fallback for removing students who are creating a disturbance from class, effective administrative interventions are designed to get students back in the classroom as quickly as possible with needed instruction and reinforcement of improved behavior. After teaching and providing opportunities to practice positive alternatives to the misbehavior that resulted in the student being sent to the office, administrators give meaningful rationales and reinforcers for using the new targeted alternatives. Students are also taught the behaviors needed to reconcile with their teachers: for example, how to apologize to their teacher for the misbehavior that resulted in an office referral. An appropriate apol-

> **Effective administrative interventions are designed to get students back in the classroom as quickly as possible with the needed instruction and with reinforcement of improved behavior.**

ogy includes looking directly at the teacher, using an appropriate tone of voice, delivering a statement that the student is sorry for the specific inappropriate behavior, and explaining the socially appropriate behavior to be used in similar situations in the future. Then the student should ask whether he or she may return to class. It is important that the school administrator conducting the intervention prepare the classroom teacher to receive the student's apology (see Black & Downs).

While this procedure is often considered to be a Tier 2 or Tier 3 intervention, it may also be a valuable part of a Tier 1 intervention plan, as it can be used with any student in the entire school, not just those who have been identified as at risk. Many students might receive the intervention only once during the school year, but for students who repeat the same problem behavior the procedure becomes more specific and is monitored over time, as typical for Tier 2 and Tier 3 interventions.

If administrative interventions are to be fully effective at the schoolwide level, procedures and expectations must be clearly communicated to faculty and students prior to implementation. Teachers and students should know in advance what the administrator will do, and what is expected of them, if a student is sent to the office. At the administrative as well as classroom level, it is best to use preventative teaching procedures rather than punishing interventions. Students and teachers must be able to clearly see the benefits of having students return to class as quickly as possible. Administrative interventions are discussed in more depth in Chapters 8 and 9, which address more individualized interventions.

SUMMARY

This chapter has explored Tier 1 (universal-level) SWPBS prevention and early intervention, including the importance of establishing schoolwide expectations for student behavior and some of the challenges involved with creating such expectations in secondary schools. Schoolwide rules were reviewed, along with guidelines to follow when creating them. The importance of proactively teaching social skills to all students was emphasized as an essential element of Tier 1 interventions. Reinforcing students' behaviors through the use of schoolwide encouragement, praise, and token economy systems was also discussed. If secondary school administrators and teachers follow these empirically based strategies, they will likely eliminate 80% of behavior problems in their schools. However, to confirm results of Tier 1 interventions they need to monitor data and use problem-solving models—topics covered in the following chapter.

FORM 5.1.

Sample of a School Praise Note

_____

Middle School

_____

Student Name

**You have been CAUGHT showing your
SCHOLAR PRIDE!**

Thank you for making our school a better place by using your social skills:

☐ How to Follow Directions

☐ How to Accept Feedback/Consequences

☐ How to Show Appreciation

☐ Other

_____   _____   _____
Signed   Date   Homeroom
_____

CHAPTER 6

Monitoring Implementation and Outcomes Using Data

In an SWPBS team meeting at Springfield High School, the teachers and administrators presented specific information about Robert, who did not seem to be responding well to Tier 1 implementation; he often skipped class and occasionally talked back to teachers. Robert had been suspended three times in the past 2 months for fighting and disorderly conduct, which included swearing and threatening violence. Robert was failing some of his classes because he was turning in only 34% of his assignments in business math. Similarly, in his sophomore English class he had completed just 46% of his assignments. His end-of-year testing from ninth grade indicated that he had below proficiency scores in language arts, mathematics, and science. His attendance was 68% during the last term. He was consistently tardy for his first-period class.

Using a problem-solving model, team members determined that Robert's difficulties were multifaceted. If Robert would consistently come to class, he would be more likely to understand and complete his assignments. However, teachers needed to be aware that Robert had below grade-level academic skills in some areas and that making adjustments in assignments and instruction could help him increase the number and accuracy of completed assignments. The team developed a plan for tracking completion of assignments, and they collaborated with Robert's parents to establish a reinforcement system contingent on assignments completed.

The team also determined that most of Robert's office referrals occurred when he was tardy the first hour. He tended to become argumentative when Mrs. Richards, his first-period teacher, confronted him about his attendance. Working with the assistant principal, Robert practiced positive, polite ways of responding to Mrs. Richards.

The team agreed to meet again in 2 weeks. Data regarding office referrals and replacement behaviors would be presented. The counselor would provide a summary of assignments completed. The parents would provide data regarding reinforcers that Robert had earned.

This example illustrates that solving problems based on data makes a significant difference in how the problem is defined and what interventions are developed. Outcomes from these

> **Using data helps teams identify interventions and resources that are needed so they can take specific steps toward progress.**

different approaches are typically better achieved. Using data helps teams identify interventions and resources that are needed so they can take specific steps toward progress. Using data also helps teams know whether their interventions are effective.

Intuitively, we know that using data to make decisions is wise and prudent. However, from experience we know that collecting and analyzing data can be a lot of work. Busy teachers do not want or need more work, especially if the additional tasks will not directly contribute to improving their teaching experiences. Among other responsibilities, teachers must complete grades, lesson plans, tracking sheets for individual students, create supplemental lessons for students who have been absent or who are behind, and respond to e-mails from parents and colleagues, as well as other tasks that take time, thought, and energy. Adding data collection tasks may seem to be asking too much.

However, the processes of collecting, analyzing, and using data are essential for the success of individual students and classrooms, as well as for schoolwide prevention and intervention efforts: the process does not have to be overly complex. Educators can be more productive when

> **Educators can be more productive when data are available to assess and monitor patterns of problem behaviors resulting in saved time by avoiding inefficient efforts.**

data are available to assess and monitor patterns of problem behaviors resulting in saved time by avoiding inefficient efforts. This chapter focuses on collecting and using data to create a process of continual, informed school improvement that helps meet the needs of both students and educators.

RECOGNIZING THE IMPORTANCE OF DATA FOR DECISION MAKING

> **An important goal of establishing SWPBS is to prevent problems from occurring and to intervene when they do occur.**

An important goal of establishing SWPBS is to prevent problems from occurring and to intervene when they do occur. Schools that have been successful in accomplishing this goal collect data to make better decisions that will help create safe and effective school environments. This process is referred to as *data-based decision making* or *problem solving*. Teams analyze data to identify problem areas and behaviors across the school and then address those problems proactively (George, Harrower, & Knoster, 2003). A simple four-step problem-solving model that can promote positive student outcomes is shown below (Florida Department of Education, 2006):

1. Problem identified in observable, behavioral terms.
2. Plan development based on the data collected.
3. Plan implementation with progress toward goals being monitored.
4. Evaluation using data to determine whether the plan is working.

Collecting data to aid in decision making has many benefits (see, e.g., McIntosh, Reinke, & Herman, 2009). Such a process helps to ensure that resources are used strategically and intentionally to address identified needs in the school rather than accessed spontaneously to respond to the latest or loudest crises. School staff can use school-level data to effectively locate particular occasions, times, and places where students need more support.

> **School staff can use school-level data to effectively locate particular occasions, times, and places where students need more support.**

Subsequent data can be used to determine whether the approaches to solving behavioral problems are effective. McIntosh et al. described three basic questions, along with subquestions, to consider when collecting data for decision making (p. 137):

1. Is the current approach achieving the intended outcomes?
   - Is the plan working as well as or better than it did last year?
   - Is a change in the plan needed?
   - Do students have the skills to do what is expected?
   - Are the behavioral needs of all students being adequately met?
2. What areas need improvement?
   - Which grade levels need additional skills training?
   - What physical areas of the school are perceived as less safe?
   - Which classroom routines do students need to be retaught?
3. Which students need additional support?
   - Which students received two or more ODRs in the first month of school?
   - Which students consistently show signs of emotional distress (e.g., anxiety, depression)?

These questions can help teams (1) determine clear goals for their interventions, and then (2) design appropriate systems to determine whether the goals have been achieved. Effective changes can only be made when problem areas and behaviors are identified and understood. Sustainability is more likely to be achieved if data are used to inform decisions.

> **Effective changes can only be made when problem areas and behaviors are identified and understood.**

ESTABLISHING A DATA-BASED DECISION-MAKING SYSTEM

As school teams begin to recognize the importance of making data-based decisions, questions may arise concerning how to begin establishing systems to collect and use data. Creating such processes need not be overly complex or time consuming; indeed it should be simple and efficient (Horner, Sugai, & Todd, 2001). The following points are based on suggestions provided by Horner et al. for establishing a data-based decision-making system (p. 21):

1. *Begin with the team.* Teams should frequently emphasize data to make decisions about implementing interventions and determining how well they are meeting the intended outcomes and goals.

2. *Focus on a few key outcomes.* Most schools will collect several types of information regarding student behavior. The goal is to collect information on the most important outcomes using the smallest number of data sources possible. By providing staff development sessions

to teach how data collected are linked to outcomes, teams can establish a solid foundation for decision making. For example, target outcomes could include decreasing ODRs, out-of-school suspensions, or referrals to special education teams. Other data that focus on positive outcomes might include the number of students who can state the school rules or expectations or the number who receive praise notes.

3. *Summarize data for decision makers.* Every school needs a standard system for entering and summarizing data, including support for efficient technology use. Teams need clear, concise data reports that identify patterns in student data and help them make effective discipline decisions.

George et al. (2003) suggest additional considerations. The first is that problem behaviors need to be clearly defined to school staff so there is no disagreement or misunderstanding. For example, Mrs. Oneida may write an ODR when a student threatens to beat up another student in class. In contrast, Mr. Gill may not send this student to the office unless the student actually hits the peer. Teachers have different levels of tolerance and comfort; part of training and development for teachers should include creating standardized, consistent definitions of what constitutes an ODR. Second, a data collection system should be used to track the number of discipline incidents occurring throughout the school. Without such a system the school staff is left to rely on their memory of discipline incidents, which can be unreliable and misleading. Third, data should be recorded daily, as ODRs occur, and analyzed by the school team at every meeting. If school team members are not getting regular data updates and summaries, they will not be able to make changes and improvements to the prevention and intervention efforts. Finally, whatever data are collected should be meaningful to school staff and should guide ongoing decision-making procedures in the school. Without such meaningful use of data, school staff may question the value of providing such data to administrators or teams.

> **Without such a system the school staff is left to rely on their memory of discipline incidents, which can be unreliable and misleading.**

Using a Variety of Data

A variety of data sources can be used to inform data-based decision making regarding key outcomes selected by the team. Data such as students' academic scores, attendance records, and ODRs are especially helpful because they are already collected by schools, resulting in efficient use of staff time. Schools can also add periodic student, teacher, and/or parent surveys or interviews to assess a variety of stakeholder perceptions, assisting school teams in creating targeted change within their schools.

Important information regarding patterns in student behavior problems can be identified via ODR data; surveys, interviews, and focus groups with teachers, staff, and students; and schoolwide screening for students with emotional and behavioral concerns (Marchant et al., 2009). Integrating the information gathered from such activities can aid SWPBS teams in selecting appropriate data-based schoolwide expectations. As stated by Marchant et al., "Examination of multiple sources of information appears to create a more comprehensive picture of what is happening in schools than does relying on a single data source" (p. 139). However, school teams need to ensure that the number of data sources is manageable, so they are not overwhelmed with too much information or so busy collecting data that they do not have time to review the data and implement interventions.

Using Systems Productively

Teams should review their existing data systems for accuracy, reliability, and usability, and work with school administration to make changes if needed. Teams should determine whether available systems already contain data that answer their explicit, specific questions; for example, "Did increasing supervision in the lunchroom decrease the number of ODRs during lunchtime?" or "Did the friendship group help students who are socially isolated?" Collecting data without having a definite question is like going shopping without a list. Teams may spend a great deal of effort and time collecting data and creating systems that do not give them the answers they really need.

Unfortunately, in many schools the majority of staff may not have experience with using data and data systems and may struggle to use a good system effectively. For example, we have found that secondary school teachers may know how to write an ODR; however, many do not know how to use school data systems that monitor and summarize students' ODRs because this tends to be the role of administrators. But such use may be vital for a team that is monitoring individual student progress. In fact, inadequate training has been cited as one of the major reasons why data are not widely used by teachers and administrators (Holcomb, 2004). Thus an important component of effective SWPBS is training on the use of school data systems.

USING ODRS

ODRs are a type of data particularly well suited for data-based decision making, especially at Tier 1. ODRs can help a team to identify areas for interventions and to measure the impact of those interventions. An ODR can be defined as follows:

> **ODRs can help a team to identify areas for interventions and to measure the impact of those interventions.**

> An event where 1) a student engaged in a behavior that violated a rule/social norm in the school, 2) a problem behavior was observed by a member of the school staff, and 3) the event resulted in a consequence delivered by administrative staff who produced a permanent (written) product defining the whole event. (Sprague, Sugai, Horner, & Walker, 1999, p. 8)

Implementing an ODR System

While most secondary schools have an ODR system in place, these systems may not be ideally designed to assist school teams in monitoring SWPBS implementation. It is important that an ODR system have agreed-upon and clear definitions of behaviors that warrant a student being sent to the office. Table 6.1 has examples of problem behaviors with clear definitions. An agreed-upon ODR form is also necessary with such critical information as the

> **It is important that an ODR system have agreed-upon and clear definitions of behaviors that warrant a student being sent to the office.**

TABLE 6.1. Sample Problem Behaviors with Clear Definitions

Problem behaviors	Definitions
Abusive language/profanity	Use of inappropriate language including swearing, cursing, name calling
Defiance	Refusal to follow directions
Disrespect	Talking back and/or socially rude interactions
Noncompliance	Failure to respond to adult requests
Physical aggression	Physical contact with potential for injury including hitting, punching, kicking, throwing of objects
Physical contact	Inappropriate physical touch including pinching, poking, tapping, grabbing

student's name, who referred the student, the date, time, and location of the incident, along with what the staff member did and how the student reacted. See Form 6.1 (at the end of the chapter) for a sample ODR form.

Systems exist for efficiently implementing and tracking ODRs, which can be used by planning teams. For example, the School-Wide Information System (SWIS; *www.swis.org*), is a secure Web-based data management system that allows school staff to enter and monitor ODR data. SWIS can be used to create numerical reports and to characterize individual or school-wide discipline. SWPBS teams can use the information provided by SWIS to make data-based decisions.

With SWIS, information can be quickly and easily compiled into charts depicting behavioral data in various ways (e.g., types of behavior leading to referral, time or setting of referrals). SWIS can also provide information about behavioral needs of individual students or groups of students. Additionally, the program can help school staff assess the percentage of students at each of the three tiers (e.g., what percentage of students are getting zero or one ODR, two to four ODRs, five or more ODRs), the number of suspension days for a given student or for groups of students, and the rate of ODRs for students with disabilities (Lindsey & White, 2010).

If school personnel are interested in using SWIS, they need to be aware of the possibility that some school districts have their own ODR data management systems already in place, and schools within the district may be required to record ODR data in these systems. They may have to enter ODR data twice: once in the district system and again in SWIS. Working with the school district administration to brainstorm possible solutions may help alleviate this problem.

When a decision is made to use SWIS, a facilitator is initially assigned to work with school personnel. The facilitator reviews a "readiness checklist" with the principal and another member of the school team, covering some basic SWPBS principles that need to be in place, such as systems for reporting behavioral issues, shared definitions of behavioral expectations, and alignment of school discipline with SWIS. An initial training occurs after the school meets the readiness criteria and the subscription is completed. The facilitator continues to work with the school through the first few months to help personnel use the collected data for decision making. At present a subscription to SWIS costs $250 per year.

Systems like SWIS can help make collecting behavioral data more simple, quick, and efficient. On average, inputting an ODR into SWIS takes just 45 seconds (Lindsey & White, 2010). Correctly interpreting such data can help better predict students' patterns of delinquent behavior and their potential to commit aggressive acts against peers and others (Tobin, Sugai, & Colvin, 2000). If students do have such externalizing behaviors, they can be identified early, be closely monitored, and be referred to Tier 2 or Tier 3 interventions if needed. We now discuss how school teams might use ODR data to monitor interventions, review the strengths and weaknesses of ODRs, and provide case studies of ODR use in Tier 1 interventions.

Using ODR Data to Monitor Interventions

There are several ways in which ODRs can be used by school teams that meet to review data displays, as noted by Clonan, McDougal, Clark, and Davison (2007, pp. 21–23):

• *ODRs by month.* Analyzing ODRs every month (or even more frequently if possible) allows teams to respond to the data in a timely manner. If ODRs increase in a given month, the team can seek to determine what caused the increase and which students, settings, teachers, and/or grade levels should be the focus of intervention efforts. See Figure 6.1 for a sample graph of ODRs by month.

• *ODRs by infraction.* ODR graphs can display results by behavioral infractions. The most common and problematic behaviors can be easily identified, and interventions specific to those behaviors can be implemented. See Figure 6.2 for a sample graph of ODRs by type of infraction.

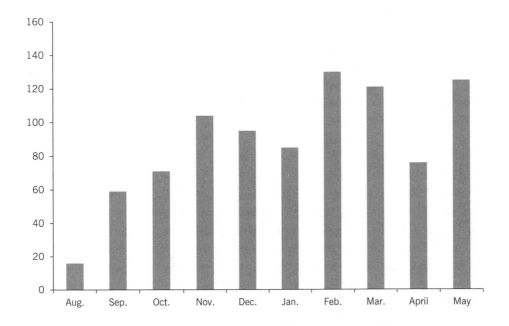

FIGURE 6.1. Sample graph illustrating total number of ODRs by month.

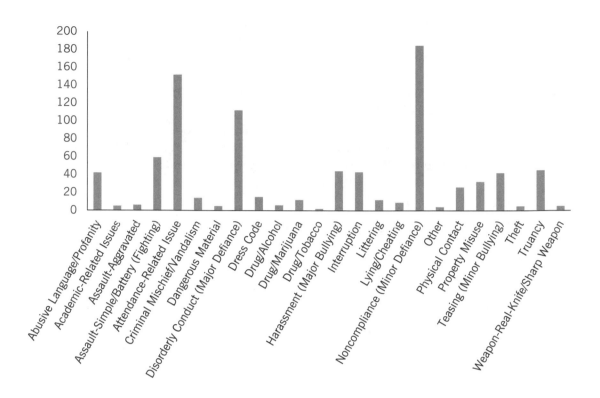

FIGURE 6.2. Sample graph illustrating total number of ODRs by type of infraction.

• *ODRs by location.* Identifying the most common locations of behavioral infractions in the school allows school teams to focus intervention efforts in those locations. See Figure 6.3 for a sample graph of ODRs by location.

• *ODRs by student.* Identifying students who have received more than one ODR during the school year can help teams recognize the ones who may need more individualized and intensive behavioral interventions. Assessing student ODRs early in the school year may also be a tool to measure the effectiveness of the interventions for a particular student or small group of students throughout the rest of the year.

> Identifying students who have received more than one ODR during the school year can help teams recognize the ones who may need more individualized and intensive behavioral interventions.

• *ODRs by grade and/or staff member.* If a specific grade level or staff member records a high number of ODRs, increased interventions may be needed for students, with additional support and/or professional development for staff members.

Sadler (2000) provided the following examples of the use of ODRs in secondary schools: One middle school team discovered 50 to 80% of its ODRs were coming from classrooms. Given these data, the team arranged for increased classroom management support for their teachers. Another middle school team implemented a lunch activity program and noticed that ODRs dur-

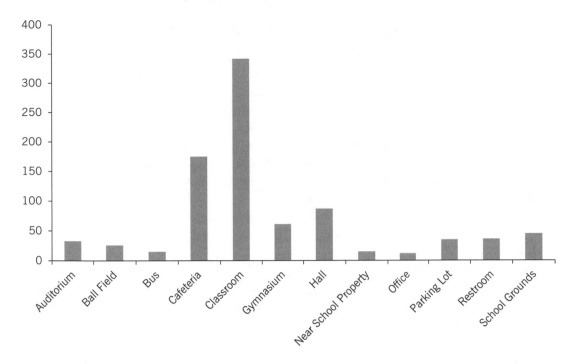

FIGURE 6.3. Sample graph illustrating total number of ODRs by location.

ing lunchtime decreased from 10% in the fall of 1998 to 4% in the fall of 1999. Mass-Galloway, Panyan, Smith, and Wessendorf (2008) reported the evaluation from a SWPBS initiative in Iowa starting in 2002, which saw a 42% decrease of ODRs per day per 100 students across a 2-year period in 24 participating schools. The amount of time saved by these ODR reductions included 10 minutes of administrator's time per referral and 20 minutes of instructional time per referral. In fact, one school in which ODRs were tracked saved 239.3 hours of instructional time and 119.6 hours of administrator time over 3 years.

ODRs are also useful for considering the consistency of application of school discipline policies. For example, if talking back to a teacher results in an ODR in Mr. Hansen's class but not in Mrs. Norton's class, then behavioral expectations and discipline

> **ODRs are also useful for considering the consistency of application of school discipline policies.**

procedures may not be consistent in the school. This inconsistency may lead to confusion and frustration among the school community. Both students and teachers need to understand which behaviors will result in an ODR, regardless of the setting. A good example was provided by Morgan-D'Atrio, Northup, LaFleur, and Spera (1996) where school staff used a summary report of ODRs to determine that approximately 45% of the disciplinary actions in the school did not correspond to the written policies and that 20% of the suspensions violated those policies. For example, some students were suspended although the school discipline policy did not include suspension as an acceptable consequence for their misbehavior. Administrators and teachers must work together to avoid such problems and come to consensus as they use data to monitor schoolwide intervention efforts.

Recognizing Strengths and Weaknesses of ODR Data

Some of the advantages noted in the literature concerning use of ODRs include the fact that they are a record of real-time interactions in schools (Tobin, Lewis-Palmer, & Sugai, 2002; Wright & Dusek, 1998) and a potentially easy accessible measure of school climate and student behavior as noted in Chapter 3. They are an inexpensive and efficient source of data already used by schools that can help identify problem behavior patterns and provide frequency counts of these behaviors (Sprague et al., 1999; Sugai, Lewis-Palmer, Todd, & Horner, 2001; Tobin et al., 2002; Wright & Dusek, 1998). The quality of discipline systems within schools can also be evaluated using ODR data: ODRs provide information to document whether schoolwide interventions are resulting in positive changes (Sprague et al.).

> **Although ODRs offer many advantages, they do have some limitations.**

Although ODRs offer many advantages, they do have some limitations. First, as we have mentioned, teachers may have biases and variations in their tolerance for students' behavior; thus ODRs may not represent independent or objective behavioral data (Clonan et al., 2007). ODRs may be associated with both high false positive rates (signaling problems that do not really exist) and high false negative rates (failing to detect problems that do exist; Nelson, Gonzales, Epstein, & Benner, 2003). Many schools have unique ways of applying ODR procedures (Sprague et al., 1999), so comparisons across schools may be difficult. ODRs also require that teachers, students, and administrators take time to complete and process. Finally, ODRs do not typically indentify students with internalizing behaviors (e.g., anxiety and depression). Despite these limitations, we believe that the advantages of using ODRs as a data source outweigh their weaknesses.

ATTENDING TO TREATMENT FIDELITY

Data can be collected for a variety of purposes beyond determining what interventions are needed and whether the interventions worked. In this section we address the importance of

> **When interventions are designed, attending to treatment fidelity is critical.**

using data to track treatment fidelity, an essential component of SWPBS implementation. When interventions are designed, attending to treatment fidelity is critical.

Meaning of Treatment Fidelity

Whether the intervention was implemented as designed is referred to as *treatment fidelity*. This match between plan and reality affects the strength of the intervention—enabling the team to evaluate processes and monitor outcomes. For example, the intervention team decided to praise and encourage Susanna, a student who demonstrated withdrawn, shy behaviors each time she was asked or expected to answer a question in class. After 3 weeks the team met to evaluate progress. Unfortunately, the teacher reported that she had not noticed much improvement in Susanna's class participation. When the team discussed reasons why there was little progress, they recognized that the teacher had so many other things going on in her classroom she forgot to praise and encourage Susanna and record the number of times that she did so. The team concluded that the intervention had not been delivered as intended. Rather than concluding that the intervention did not work, the team should return to the problem-solving process and consider modifications to this intervention or other interventions that are more likely to be implemented with integrity.

By evaluating treatment fidelity, school teams can accurately determine the potential effect an intervention will have on student behavior and then make adjustments if needed. Mihalic (2004) outlines several components to think about when considering treatment fidelity:

- *Adherence* refers to whether the intervention is being delivered as it was designed or written.
- *Exposure* may include the number of interventions implemented, length of each intervention, or number of times the intervention was implemented.
- *Quality of program delivery* is the way in which a teacher or school staff member delivers an intervention.
- *Student responsiveness* is the extent to which students respond to interventions.

If treatment fidelity is not assessed, it is difficult to determine whether the intervention resulted in changes in student behavior that were consistent with the intended goals or whether the changes were related to some other cause. For example, if a teacher modifies some of the key intervention components, the modification may affect the desired outcomes. If student behavior does not change or improve, it will

> **If treatment fidelity is not assessed, it is difficult to determine whether the intervention resulted in changes in student behavior that were consistent with the intended goals or whether the changes were related to some other cause.**

be difficult to determine whether the wrong intervention was used or if the modifications in an evidence-based practice prevented an appropriate intervention from being as effective as it has been in the past. If treatment fidelity is not achieved, the problem may be that the intervention overwhelmed teachers or was not sufficiently supported by others (e.g., administrators, parents), that the teacher lacked sufficient training or resources, or that the intervention took too much time or effort to implement.

Because it is directly related to the outcomes of interventions, it is important to understand the factors that will produce a high level of treatment fidelity. The following factors should be considered when designing interventions to ensure high levels of treatment fidelity (see Lane & Beebe-Frankenberger, 2004):

- *Complexity and time commitments.* Generally as interventions become more complex and time consuming, the level of treatment fidelity decreases.
- *Materials required.* The more materials and resources required for implementing an intervention, the lower the treatment fidelity, especially if the required materials and resources are not available within the classroom.
- *Number of staff involved.* If interventions require assistance from more than one person, they will likely have lower levels of treatment fidelity compared to interventions that require a single individual.
- *Perceived and actual effectiveness.* If the person implementing an intervention (usually the teacher) believes it will be effective or socially valid (i.e., socially appropriate and acceptable), he or she will be more likely to implement it as planned.

Assessing Treatment Fidelity

> Since treatment fidelity is such an important aspect of designing and evaluating interventions, an implementation team must understand how it can be assessed in schools.

Since treatment fidelity is such an important aspect of designing and evaluating interventions, an implementation team must understand how it can be assessed in schools. A number of strategies can be used. We focus first on several measurement suggestions given by Lane and Beebe-Frankenberger (2004):

- *Direct observation.* A detailed list of intervention components is created, and an observer watches interventions as they occur, paying attention to the presence of components and nature of student responses. While this is more common in research settings, schools may be able to use trained and supervised school volunteers to perform such observations.
- *Feedback from consultants.* A consultant who is trained in the intervention components, but is not participating in implementing the intervention observes the school staff during implementation and provides corrective feedback. More frequent feedback can result in higher levels of treatment fidelity.
- *Self-monitoring.* Teachers can record data on how well they implemented the intervention. Teachers can also speak with a consultant, administrator, or other member of the school staff about each individual component of an intervention and share the self-monitoring data they collected. These data should be discussed with others because an outsider may be able to discern when claimed treatment fidelity may not be valid.
- *Manualized treatments and intervention scripts.* Interventions containing components such as scripted lessons may be implemented with greater fidelity because they can help clarify behavior expectations for the teachers and students. Intervention scripts can also aid assessment of treatment fidelity because teachers and/or outside observers can use them in deciding whether each intervention component is present.

> Interventions containing components such as scripted lessons may be implemented with greater fidelity because they can help clarify behavior expectations for the teachers and students.

Any of these strategies can be used singly or with others to assess the level of treatment fidelity within a school. Assessment of treatment fidelity will be individualized to schools, and teams will have to collaborate with administration and outside consultants to determine which assessment techniques will be best to use.

The School-Wide Evaluation Tool (SET; Sugai et al., 2001) is another useful measure for evaluating treatment fidelity. The SET was designed to specifically measure the degree to which schools are implementing important features of SWPBS. This tool is available free of charge on the Positive Behavioral Intervention and Supports website (*www.pbis.org/evaluation/evaluation_tools.aspx*), as is a companion implementation manual that provides an overview of the SET, gives good examples of how to effectively score it, and explains how schools can prepare to conduct a SET assessment. The SET is usually completed once a year by a trained observer who assesses the following seven important SWPBS features (Bradshaw, Reinke, Brown, & Leaf, 2008, p. 3):

1. *Expectations defined*. Three to five positive schoolwide behavior expectations are defined and posted in high traffic areas throughout the school.
2. *Behavior expectations taught*. Each behavior expectation is taught to every student in the school.
3. *Reward system for behavioral expectations established*. Rewards are provided to students who meet the school's behavior expectations.
4. *System for responding to behavioral violations in place*. Consistent consequences are in place for students who do not comply with behavior expectations.
5. *Monitoring and evaluation determined*. Behavior patterns are monitored by school staff, and the data collected are used by teams for ongoing decision making.
6. *Management implemented*. A school administrator is actively involved in SWPBS efforts, and a team is formed.
7. *District-level support obtained*. The school district provides support to the school with functional policies, staff training, and data collection procedures.

The SET has 29 items, which are organized into subscales that correspond with the seven core SWPBS features. Each SET item is scored on a 3-point Likert-type scale (i.e., 0 = *not implemented*, 1 = *partial implementation*, and 2 = *full implementation*). The seven subscales are measured as ranging from 0 to 100%, with a higher percentage indicating greater levels of treatment fidelity. An overall summary score can be calculated by averaging all of the subscale scores. The developers of SET assert that when SWPBS components have reached at least 80% fidelity, the program will produce the intended outcomes as planned (Bradshaw et al., 2008).

During a SET assessment, a trained observer determines how well a school has each of the SET's seven features in place. He or she can make this determination by reviewing written materials and established discipline procedures, such as school improvement goals and ODR procedures, and by noting visual displays of the school's behavior expectations throughout the school. Assessors can also hold interviews with administrators, school staff, and students about school policies and behavior standards (Mass-Galloway et al., 2008).

Even with a SET assessment, in the end the success or failure of behavioral interventions depends on how accurately and consistently teachers implement the interventions. Adequate training and consistent support for teachers who will implement the intervention are critical. It is also important to assess the social validity of interventions, as this can impact treatment fidelity and the success or failure of schoolwide efforts.

> In the end the success or failure of behavioral interventions depends on how accurately and consistently teachers implement the interventions.

UNDERSTANDING SOCIAL VALIDITY

As school personnel strive to implement schoolwide interventions, they must consider social validity (Finn & Sladeczek, 2001), which means that participants should evaluate the intervention goals and procedures as socially appropriate and acceptable. Additionally, the effects or outcomes of the intervention should be judged as socially significant.

Social validity takes on slightly different meanings at different stages of intervention implementation, as noted by Lane and Beebe-Frankenberger (2004). Before implementing an intervention, school teams should ask the following: Will achieving the intervention goal improve the students' quality of life? Does the goal of the intervention have social value? Social acceptability of interventions must be assessed prior to implementing them in order to ensure that the targeted outcomes are worth the effort required. Since an intervention with social validity has greater likelihood of being implemented with treatment fidelity, the level of buy-in from staff and parents must be understood from the beginning. It might be helpful to ask why teachers do not find the intervention (or parts of the intervention) acceptable, what is missing, and what can be done to improve the process.

Social validity of the intervention can also be assessed at the end of the intervention to determine whether it has produced meaningful, lasting changes in student behavior and whether those changes have been worth the effort to achieve. School teams should ask whether implementation procedures were necessary and appropriate, whether the intervention enhanced the school environment, and whether students' ability to demonstrate appropriate school behavior was improved.

Measuring Social Validity

Social validity can be measured through a variety of methods including the use of surveys and interview techniques. Surveys often involve questionnaires on which school staff rate statements or questions as to the fairness and expected effectiveness of intervention procedures, using a Likert-type scale. School staff and parents can also use rating scales to assess how interventions have affected outcomes (Finn & Sladeczek, 2001). Formal or informal interviews can be used individually or with groups to assess social validity. Schools are advised to include interview techniques only when team members have the skills and experience to adequately evaluate qualitative interview data. Summarizing and analyzing interview data also tends to take more time and expertise than evaluating survey data. All of the above measures can also be used with students to obtain their perceptions regarding the social validity of interventions.

Lane et al. (2009) provide an example of how a school district measured social validity and its effect on treatment fidelity. The district assessed the social validity of SWPBS programs before beginning interventions. During a faculty meeting school teams distributed handouts outlining the major goals and behavioral expectations of the SWPBS plan. At the end of the meeting teachers completed an anonymous survey to assess the social validity of the proposed plan (i.e., the social significance of the intervention goals, the social acceptability of intervention procedures, and the likelihood of socially important outcomes). Findings suggested that social validity ratings collected before implementing the interventions predicted the level of treatment fidelity during the first year of SWPBS implementation. Schools can use similar procedures for assessing the social validity of their own SWPBS programs.

> **Findings suggested that social validity ratings collected before implementing the interventions predicted the level of treatment fidelity during the first year of SWPBS implementation.**

SUMMARY

In this chapter we have addressed the importance of making data-based decisions using a variety of data sources. We have emphasized that data must be provided to school teams in order for them to improve the effectiveness and relevance of intervention efforts. ODRs were noted as being particularly effective in assisting school teams in making data-based decisions regarding student behavior. Treatment integrity and social validity were explained, along with suggestions for assessment. Even when a school has completed all of these tasks, some students will still need more than Tier 1 supports; correctly identifying these students through systematic screening is the topic of the next chapter.

Office Discipline Referral Form

Student

Name: _____ Grade: _____

Date: _____ Time: _____

Problem Behavior:

_____

Location/Context:

_____

Interventions Tried:

_____

Student Response:

_____

Referred by:

_____

Others Involved:

_____

Administrative Action
Action Taken:

_____

Follow-Up Needed:

_____

Notified Parent/Guardian

Who: _____ How: _____

Date: _____ Time: _____

Comments:

CHAPTER 7

Schoolwide Screening

When Mr. Terry reviewed his daughter's end-of-semester report card, he was dismayed. Nichole, a ninth grader at Elms Junior High, had earned mostly C's and B's during the first 9 weeks of the year. During the second 9 weeks, her grades dropped to mostly D's. She had had 89% attendance during the first term, but only 63% attendance during the second term. Her English, math, and science teachers noticed the drop in grades, and each teacher spoke individually with her father during parent–teacher conferences. He agreed to talk with Nichole and see whether they could work together to improve her grades and attendance. He indicated there was no medical reason for her excessive absences; he did not realize she had missed that much school.

Several days after parent–teacher conferences, the physical education teacher casually mentioned to the school counselor that something didn't seem quite right with Nichole. She didn't appear to interact with the other students during group activities. At times she seemed withdrawn and rarely talked or joined in with the other girls in the class. During the various games the class was learning, Nichole seemed to disappear into the woodwork.

The counselor shared this concern with the art teacher hoping to get her perspective about Nichole's behavior and schoolwork. The art teacher hadn't noticed any particular problems, but hadn't specifically looked at Nichole's grades; Nichole was not a behavior problem in class.

The school counselor was concerned about Nichole, but there were no really big problems: she wasn't failing classes yet; she wasn't being suspended; her attendance was a concern. There were certainly other students with more severe problems. The counselor decided to wait for a couple of weeks to see whether Nichole's grades, attendance, and withdrawn behaviors improved.

As the school year moved on the teachers continued to be concerned about Nichole, but because they didn't have processes in place for identifying and meeting the needs of at-risk students, no actions were taken. Nichole's father assumed that Nichole was doing sufficiently well in school since he did not hear any additional concerns from the teachers.

When the school year ended, Nichole had failed most of her classes, had few friends, and was described as very withdrawn and isolated. Realizing the extent of the problems at the end of the year, her father began looking for a counselor who could help him understand why Nichole was having problems. At an end-of-the year meeting, her teachers expressed regret for not doing something to address the concerns they had observed.

OVERVIEW OF SCREENING

Screening for behavioral and emotional concerns for secondary students casts a wide net to identify students who need emotional, behavioral, and academic support. Effective screening helps to identify and address potential problems before they become so extensive and maladaptive that they are difficult and expensive to remediate. Screening is an integral part of developing and maintaining a continuum of services for students with emotional and behavioral difficulties.

> **Effective screening helps to identify and address potential problems before they become so extensive and maladaptive that they are difficult and expensive to remediate.**

Purposes of Screening

When there is a continuum of services, screening is necessary to discern which students need the various available interventions. Without screening, some students in need may not receive any services; others may be assigned to inappropriate or inadequate interventions, and the desired outcomes will not be achieved. Data generated by the screening process can also inform the types of interventions that are needed in a school. Developing prevention and early intervention services are important outcomes of a screening process.

Screening is different from diagnosing in both purposes and outcomes. Diagnosing is done at the individual level to determine a specific disorder such as depression, anxiety, attention-deficit/hyperactivity disorder (ADHD), learning disabilities, or autism. The assessment process results in a conclusive label, identification, or diagnostic category from which to develop a precise diagnosis. The diagnostic process tends to be time and resource intensive, and is focused on individuals who have specific long-standing problems and will probably need individual interventions. Detailed assessment should also focus on gaining the information needed to develop responsive, typically individual, interventions (Glover & Albers, 2007).

Screening is intended to identify students who exhibit risk factors for academic or emotional difficulties and to develop interventions that will prevent risk factors from turning into full-blown disorders. At the "risk" level, labeling the students with a diagnosis or special education classification is not appropriate because their social or academic behavior problems are not yet significant enough to warrant a definitive diagnosis. Screening can indicate students who have some (but not all) symptoms of a disorder or some risk factors that often lead to school failure or significant mental health problems. Screening is focused on early identification of concerns to prevent more serious problems; this process requires less time than diagnosis and while it is used to identify students with special needs, it also identifies groups of students who may need intervention in the general education setting. School-based screening tends to focus on a broad range of concerns and symptoms rather than on a particular disorder such as depression or substance abuse.

> **Screening is different from diagnosing in both purposes and outcomes. Diagnosing is done at the individual level to determine a specific disorder.**

Identifying students like Nichole before they fail helps school teams and families find solutions before the situation seems overwhelming and hopeless. When problems are identified early there are usually more options and resources for addressing the difficulties. For example, because Nichole has failed some of her classes, she will need to retake them during the summer or through independent study. If her falling grades had been dealt with before she actually failed, it is possible that monitoring and support from parents and teachers could have enabled her to pass her classes. Addressing her withdrawn behaviors during the school year through a variety of interventions would have facilitated her receiving timely, responsive services.

Uses of a Screening Process

Screening is not for the purpose of putting students in special education; rather it is a process of identifying needs and then implementing interventions to meet those needs in a general education class if possible. It is not a means of recruiting students for programs or assigning students to programs with low achievement expectations; nor is it intended to label students and put them in long-term remedial programs. Screening should not create an underclass within the school culture. Screening should be directly tied to delivering monitored evidence-based interventions that are helpful in facilitating positive change so that students can continue in the general education setting, learn needed skills, and develop competencies.

> Screening should be directly tied to delivering monitored evidence-based interventions that are helpful in facilitating positive change so that students can continue in the general education setting, learn needed skills, and develop competencies.

Prevention and early intervention is a wise use of educational resources; providing early intervention is more cost effective than reacting to fully developed disorders (Levitt, Saka, Romanelli, & Hoagwood, 2007). A comprehensive evaluation, which historically has been a major component in the special education process, is one way of identifying needs, but it tends to rely on the wait-to-fail approach rather than a proactive, preventative approach that provides interventions before failure has repeatedly occurred.

Effective screening should address a foundational question: What are we screening for (Severson, Walker, Hope-Doolittle, Kratochwill, & Gresham, 2007)? The answer to this question must consider the types and intensities of interventions available—driving decisions about what screening measure to use and how to use it and evaluate it. The results of a screening process can drive the interventions that are developed and implemented. For example, if screening reveals that more students need support in joining social groups, a short-term intervention may be developed to address social needs.

Screening is a very important part of developing and providing a continuum of services. If appropriate interventions for at-risk students are not accessible, screening is a useless process. If a screening process shows evidence of serious concerns (e.g., suicidal behavior), educators and professionals have an ethical obligation to address those needs or help the student and family find resources to resolve them. Screening provides information but if that information is not used to improve services for students, why spend the time to gather the information? If teams work diligently to develop tiered interventions but then do not have a plan for

> If teams work diligently to develop tiered interventions but then do not have a plan for identifying students who need the variety of services offered, their efforts may not achieve the intended outcomes.

identifying students who need the variety of services offered, their efforts may not achieve the intended outcomes.

The Role of Screening in General Education

In the general education population, students tend to have a wide variety of emotional and behavioral concerns; their problems occur along a continuum, and a variety of resources are needed to meet their needs (Ringeisen, Henderson, & Hoagwood, 2003). Screening helps identify these students and their needs so that appropriate intervention services can be implemented in the general education setting. For example, some students may need to be included in a "friendshipping" group; others may benefit from a short-term intervention teaching self-monitoring skills for independently completing assignments; students with frequent absences may need incentives or other supports to increase attendance. Youth who are experiencing frequent ODRs may require help in learning alternative conflict management skills or other social skills. Others may need supplementary instruction and practice to learn a difficult math concept or improve writing skills.

Problem Identification

Screening and diagnosing are qualitatively different processes with different outcomes and purposes. The point of screening is to identify students who are at risk for a problem or who have troubling behaviors. Screening facilitates early intervention and provides a timely response for addressing current behavioral and emotional issues. An evaluation may result in a specific label, such as depression, anxiety, or a learning disability; an individual psychoeducational evaluation has typically been completed to determine special education eligibility by identifying students with educational disabilities that integrates information from a variety of sources and measures. Screening is usually a less time-intensive process than a complete individual evaluation.

General education teachers are usually well qualified to identify the early risk factors for behavioral problems that are the focus of screening; however, a systematic process to gather teachers' perceptions of student problems occurs infrequently. Teachers have a wealth of knowledge about the social, emotional, and academic context of youth (Walker & Severson, 1992). Teachers in secondary settings have plenty of opportunities to observe students and compare behaviors among groups of students (Caldarella et al., 2008; Richardson et al., 2009). Teachers are often aware when problems are emerging because they can observe when a student has behaviors or emotions that are notably different from his or her peers.

Screening processes can also make administrators and teachers aware of students with significant needs who should be given individual evaluations that focus on developing interventions. When faculty members have significant concerns about students, a comprehensive psychoeducational evaluation is an appropriate option to consider. Federal special education mandates require that an individual evaluation should be administered only after interventions have been completed and data gathered about the effectiveness of those interventions. Some formal evaluations (e.g., IQ test, standardized achievement, behavior rating scales) tend to lack information about specific interventions that are needed; instead, this type of evaluation tends to focus on a *yes–no* special education eligibility decision with some, but not extensive, information about needed interventions.

Tiered Interventions and Screening

Screening can also provide insights about the effectiveness of a school's Tier 1 interventions (Marchant et al.,
2009). When school teams review the results of screening processes, they may consider what the data reveal
about Tier 1 interventions. For example, if many stu-

> **Screening can also provide insights about the effectiveness of a school's Tier 1 interventions.**

dents are being identified because they have excessive ODRs for disorderly conduct, the team
may consider the possibility that schoolwide expectations for respectful, appropriate behavior
may not be clearly communicated to or understood by students, and thus a strategy for explicitly
teaching and rewarding respectful behavior is needed. If the results of screening indicate that
many students have internalizing behaviors, such as depression, social isolation, or anxiety, a
schoolwide curriculum on healthy emotions may be appropriate (e.g., Herman, Merrell, Reinke,
& Tucker, 2004; Merrell, 2007a, 2007b).

In the vignette about Nichole, a screening process might have identified her significant
grade drop, attendance decline, and behavioral withdrawal. Her teachers could have worked
together and with her parents to determine why her grades were dropping and what could be
done to increase her attendance. Nichole could have attended a social skills group to help her
make friends and feel socially included. She could have been put on a tracking system that would
have notified her parents and teachers that she needed additional help completing assignments.
Her progress could have been monitored and actions taken before she failed ninth grade.

The Role of Screening in Preventing Mental and Emotional Health Problems

About 20% of the adolescent population has a mental health, behavioral, or emotional disorder (National Research Council and Institute of Medicine, 2009). However, only about 1% of
students are identified as having a behavior disorder and served through special education
programs that address their social, emotional, and behavioral needs (Wagner, Kutash, Duchnowski, Epstein, & Sumi, 2005). Hence, a large number of youth have emotional and behavioral
concerns that are not being met. Certainly not all youth with emotional, behavioral, or mental
health concerns can or should be served through special education, but a notable number of
students would benefit from some other types of intervention. Furthermore, attending to students' behavioral and emotional needs may promote academic competence and prevent some
of the common negative outcomes from unaddressed mental health needs (Zins, Bloodworth,
Weissberg, & Walberg, 2007). Screening is an important way to identify those students whose
needs are not being met in the general education setting.

Identifying needs through though screening and then meeting these needs before youth
are identified as a student with an emotional–behavioral disability (EBD) is intended to prevent
a range of negative outcomes. Some of the negative outcomes include about a 50% dropout rate
for students identified as EBD, the highest dropout rate of any category of educational disability.
A probable contributing factor to this high dropout rate is the likelihood of students with EBD
to have low grades and fail classes. Although 22% of students in general education have a history
of suspension or expulsion, 73% of students with EBD have records of suspensions (Wagner et
al., 2005). Lane, Carter, Pierson, and Glaeser (2006) reported that students with EBD are more

likely to miss school than other students. They tend to have academic difficulties due to poor task completion, academic skill deficits, and lack of content knowledge (Lane, Wehby, & Barton-Arwood, 2005). If interventions for these students had begun before problems become severe, the negative outcomes could likely be moderated. In fact, interventions should improve not only behavioral and emotional functioning, but also active academic engagement (Reddy, Newman, De Thomas, & Chun, 2009).

CHARACTERISTICS OF EFFECTIVE SCREENING

Screening should not be cumbersome, complex, and extraneous, but rather it should be efficiently integrated into the school culture.

Screening should be an efficient process that does not consume extensive amounts of teacher and staff time. Resource use should be focused on first identifying students who need interventions and then providing interventions that match the identified needs. Screening should not be cumbersome, complex, or extraneous, but rather it should be efficiently integrated into the school culture. Exemplary screening practices include all students in the first stage or gate and have several gates or stages. Processes that are efficient, align with interventions, technically adequate, and are repeated frequently are considered best practices.

Universal Scope

The first level of all screening processes should consider all students, including those with both internalizing and externalizing concerns (Walker & Severson, 1992). Internalizing behaviors are directed inward, such as appearing fearful or anxious, withdrawing from social interactions, having a flat affect, or demonstrating low activity levels. Students with internalizing concerns are often overlooked and typically have deficits in behavioral skills. Externalizing behaviors are directed outward and typically include behaving aggressively, failing to respond to adult requests, arguing, disrupting, and demonstrating behavioral excesses.

Some screening processes may only target students with failing grades, suicide risk, or antisocial behavior, and implementation of multiple screeners for different issues may exhaust the resources of the school. The goal of a universal screening process is to help the faculty see students' needs holistically and provide interventions that are responsive to students' needs rather than focusing on the label of the problems.

For example, completing separate screenings for depression, anxiety, social isolation, aggression, bullying, substance abuse, academic problems, dropout risk, or frequent discipline problems would require much faculty time. Use of multiple screenings with different foci also risks delivering fragmented services.

In contrast we are recommending a screening process that aligns with providing tiered interventions for a variety of emotional, behavioral, social, and academic issues. Note that the term *tiered interventions* does not just refer just to the location where an intervention may be delivered but to the level of intensity and complexity of the intervention. The results of the screening instruments may show that a group of students is experiencing problems making friends and integrating socially into the school culture, which could be due to a variety of causes. The team could help organize a 6-week social skills group that targets teaching students to start a conversation, join in an activity, and give a compliment, a typical Tier 2 intervention. Such an intervention could be delivered in the general education class by a teacher or in a small group directed by a school psychologist. As another example, students with 15 or more ODRs could participate in a different Tier 2 intervention that teaches conflict resolution. Other examples of Tier 2 interventions are discussed in Chapter 8. When students with excessive needs are identified, the team may decide that more information is needed to provide Tier 3 interventions. Chapter 9 discusses how to complete an FBA to develop more intensive and complex individualized interventions.

Repeated and Continuous

A schoolwide screening process that considers every student in the school at a particular point in time might only occur at the beginning or end of a school year; however, we should not consider the identification of students with unique needs to be a one-time event that is completed and not revisited. Screening data collection coupled with providing tailored interventions is a process of providing timely services for students who are at risk as soon as the student is identified. Screening should be perceived

> **We should not consider the identification of students with unique needs to be a one-time event that is completed and not revisited.**

as a continuous process. If a parent brings extensive concerns about his or her child's problematic behaviors between screening dates and the data might indicate that interventions are warranted, there is no need to wait until the next scheduled formal screening. If the school has a culture of continuous evaluation and support for students, identifying students with needs will be perceived by the faculty and parents as an integral part of the way the school does business.

Screening should be completed after the teachers have enough time to observe students in a variety of situations: about 6 weeks into the school year usually allows sufficient opportunity for students to demonstrate their strengths and needs. Conducting another screening shortly after the beginning of the second semester (January or February) may be needed (Severson et al., 2007), as students' needs may change as the year progresses, as Nichole's did in the chapter-opening vignette.

Technically Adequate

When school teams select screening measures, it is helpful to have clear criteria for selecting instruments that may be used. Screening measures and processes should have appropriate psychometric characteristics that enable the instrument to correctly and consistently measure the risk factors. In others words, the instrument needs to be reliable and have reasonable evidence of validity for the purposes for which it is used. If you are not familiar with test construction and psychometric data, consulting someone with that expertise is recommended.

Several questions that can guide teams in determining the technical adequacy of potential screening instruments have been developed (Glover & Albers, 2007).

1. Are the norms current, characteristic of the setting, and of suitable size?
2. Does the test developer report characteristics of reliability? Are the internal consistency measures adequate? Are test–retest reliability coefficients sufficient?
3. Is there evidence of predictive validity, including sensitivity, specificity, positive predictive value, and negative predictive value?
4. Is there evidence of concurrent validity? Are scores consistent with a criterion measure?
5. Is there evidence of construct validity? Is there evidence that the measure actually assesses what it was designed to measure?
6. Is there evidence of content validity? Do the items and form appear to be suitable?

When considering screening instruments, some types of validity are especially important to consider. *Predictive validity*, a type of validity evidence that considers a variety of other qualities of an instrument, is usually determined by evaluating sensitivity, specificity, positive predictive value, and negative predictive value. Sensitivity and specificity are two important characteristics that contribute to establishing strong evidence of validity. *Sensitivity* is the percentage of individuals identified by a screening measure who also meet an established criterion for needing additional support (Levitt et al.). *Specificity* is the proportion of individuals who are correctly identified by the instrument as not needing additional interventions (Levitt et al., 2007). Test developers should explicitly address these concepts and report results of studies in the test manual.

Multigated

Effective screening processes are intentionally created to be *processes* rather than one-step events. A multigated process involves several steps with increasingly specific information being gathered at each step or gate. Gates are decision-making points that consider whether students will proceed with the process. Questions that could be asked at each gate could include the following:

1. Does this student present enough concerning behaviors that more information is needed? If yes, continue to the next gate of the screening process. If no, consider what the data reveal about which interventions are needed.
2. Are perceptions of the student consistent among teachers? Discussing the different or similar teacher perceptions can be enlightening and can help in making decisions whether additional data are needed or what data are needed.
3. Is additional information available but not included in the current discussion? Perhaps the student's cumulative school record, previous group or individual testing, report cards, attendance records, or discipline records provide sufficient data to develop interventions.

The first step in the process should be to cast a wide net and identify a broad range of students who may need intervention. This step (or gate) should include all students in the school—be universal. Subsequent gates use more specific instruments that help teams determine particular needs of fewer students. Students who are not identified at stage one are eliminated from the ongoing screening process. As students move through the additional gates, incrementally more specific information is gathered to help plan for interventions based on the intensity of the needs.

> As students move through the additional gates, incrementally more specific information is gathered to help plan for interventions based on the intensity of the needs.

Data may reveal that a student has some risk factors and requires some interventions, but not necessarily Tier 2 or 3 interventions. For example, the team may review the data from the first gate of screening and determine that a parent–teacher meeting will sufficiently address the concern, and the student does not need to be considered at the additional screening gates. However, the student outcomes should still be monitored to ensure that the concerns have been resolved. The students who met criteria at all of the gates should be those with the most pressing concerns.

The first stage of the process may identify some students who do not need interventions and who do not receive additional consideration, but if there are multiple steps in the process, subsequent information gathering will clarify concerns. Having occasional *false positives* (students who are not at risk, but tentatively identified) in the first step of screening is preferable to having *false negatives* (at-risk students who are not identified) that will not be retroactively identified at subsequent gates (Severson et al., 2007).

Integrated with Interventions

Screening should be integral to the development of interventions and match the continuum of interventions (Glover & Albers, 2007). Complex screening processes would seem counterproductive if the developed continuum of interventions is simply two tiers. The screening process needs to match the type and system of interventions (Levitt et al., 2007). For example, if the screening process showed that a large number of seventh graders were experiencing problems with internalizing behavior, the team could consider implementing an intervention for all seventh graders that targeted how to identify anxious feelings and to use cognitive strategies for dealing with worries.

Best practices would suggest that screening is an iterative process. A small-group or Tier 2 intervention that provides more opportunities for practicing skills and receiving feedback is organized when the results of screening show that a small number of seventh-grade students are likely to need more help with anxiety issues than is going to be available through an intervention for all seventh graders. When the results of the screening process guide the development of interventions, the process becomes integral to providing information about what interventions are needed in the school.

APPROVALS NEEDED FOR SCREENING

Before screening, it is imperative that school teams consult with district administrators and understand district policies regarding this type of practice so they can appropriately protect the rights of parents or guardians and students while they are proactively identifying youth who would benefit from early intervention services.

Protection of Pupil Rights Act

> How school districts interpret the federal Protection of Pupil Rights Act (PPRA) will determine *what* kind of consent is needed and *when* that consent should be sought.

How school districts interpret the federal Protection of Pupil Rights Act (PPRA) will determine *what* kind of consent is needed and *when* that consent should be sought. The PPRA requires school teams to get written parental consent before students who are minors participate in any survey or evaluation that asks for information about emotional and psychological problems that could potentially be embarrassing to the student and his or her family (Protection of Pupil Rights Amendment, n.d.). For example, if a survey asks whether a child or his or her parents are receiving mental health services, signed parental consent is required before the child participates.

Exceptions to PPRA

Teams should also be aware of situations in which PPRA is superseded or unnecessary. If the process is permitted or required by state law without parental notification, the PPRA stipulations do not apply. For example, if a state legislature funds and requires schools to administer a survey about substance use and other issues, signed parental permission would not be needed because this survey is mandated by state law. If the screening process does not ask direct questions about physical or emotional problems but focuses on feelings or behaviors (i.e., "I have been feeling grouchy" rather than "I have an anxiety disorder"), the provisions of PPRA may not be relevant (Chartier et al., 2008).

Some school districts may consider screening to be part of the normal requirements for teachers to report their concerns about individual students and identify those who might benefit from additional support and help (Birman & Chan, 2008) with no parental permission needed. Because the teacher completes the instruments, such screening may be considered part of the Child Find process that is outlined by special education law. However, if the student rather than a teacher or counselor completes the instrument, PPRA mandates most likely will apply.

Typically, parental approval is not needed for universal screening if *all* students in the school or district are considered in the process. For example, parental permission is not needed to screen for vision and hearing problems. School districts do not typically request parental permission to administer academic benchmark assessments for students. Similarly, end-of-year academic testing does not require parental permission because all students participate. On the other hand, screening or assessing for academic problems is different from screening for emotional or behavioral concerns, which parents or guardians may perceive as invasive and beyond the domain of educational institutions. The risk of a student being labeled as having emotional or behavioral concerns could be threatening to a child or parents and raise their level of concern if interventions are not identified and offered to the student.

Substantial evidence confirms that identifying and serving youth with emotional and behavioral concerns is in their best interests. Research has shown that not serving these students often results in significant negative outcomes. The risks involved in not screening and then not serving these students is greater than the potential problems of offending parents or youth (Wagner et al., 2005).

Questions to Guide Decision Making

Whether parental approvals are needed, what form they must take, and at what point in time they are needed depend on local and state mandates. School district administrators and attorneys can help school teams in addressing the following questions:

1. How do the federal Individuals with Disabilities Act (IDEA) Child Find mandates apply to universal behavioral and emotional screening? How does PPRA apply? What other local and state laws apply?
2. Is parental permission needed for teachers to complete a schoolwide screening for all students regarding behavioral and emotional issues?
3. Is passive consent acceptable? When passive consent is used, parents are notified in a letter or in a student handbook and asked to notify the school in writing if they do not want their child to participate in a particular activity. If the parents do not notify the school, the school officials assume parents have consented to the process. In other situations (e.g., research) this type of consent is discouraged.
4. As gates of the screening process are completed and individualized information is gathered, at what point should parental permission be requested and due process rights offered?
5. How can information about students be communicated confidentially?
6. How will the information be maintained in student files? Does it need to be included in student files?

EXAMPLES OF SCREENING MEASURES

Instruments

Several instruments are available for screening purposes. The instruments reviewed in this section focus on various concerns and target behaviors. When choosing a specific screening instrument, school teams should consider how the instrument meets the objectives and needs of their student body. Table 7.1 summarizes the characteristics of the measures described below.

Systematic Screening for Behavior Disorders

The Systematic Screening for Behavior Disorders (SSBD; Walker & Severson, 1992) is intended for students in grades K–6, although it has been used in middle and junior high schools with emerging evidence that it could be suitable for secondary settings (Caldarella et al., 2008; Richardson et al., 2009; Young, Sabbah, Young, Reiser, & Richardson, 2010). The SSBD is considered the gold standard of screening instruments because it is multigated, addresses both internalizing and externalizing behaviors, and includes all students through teacher nominations in the initial screening. The psychometric properties are acceptable for elementary students and it is efficient.

Unfortunately, the SSBD was not originally developed for use in secondary settings, and adaptations are needed for use with adolescents because students have multiple teachers; incorporating the nominations of several teachers can become a complex although not unmanageable

TABLE 7.1. Summary of Screening Instruments

Instrument	Overview	Completion time	Completed by	Available from	Cost
SSBD	K–6 Multigated screening instrument	20 minutes per teacher to complete the teacher nomination form	Teachers	*www. soprislearning.com*	$131.49
SSBS-2	K–12 Measure of both positive and negative social behaviors	10 minutes per student	Teachers (home version available)	*www. brookespublishing. com*	$49.95
SRSS	K–12 Classrooms are screened for seven externalizing behaviors	10–15 minutes per classroom	Teachers	*www.mepbis.org/ docs/nwp-03-22- 10-SRSS.doc* or *pgs. boisestate.edu/pbis/ SRSS-screening-too/*	no cost
BASC-2 BESS	Preschool–12 Screening of behavioral and emotional concerns and strengths	5 minutes per student	Teachers (parent and student forms available)	*www. pearsonassessments. com*	$125.05

process (see Caldarella et al., 2008). Also, the norms are now considerably out of date. If this instrument is used in secondary settings, it would be appropriate to carefully evaluate its use.

School Social Behavior Scales, Second Edition

The School Social Behavior Scales, Second Edition (SSBS-2; Merrell, 2008) address both positive social skills and antisocial behaviors. The SSBS-2 is intended for use in grades K–12, and takes about 10 minutes per student for teachers to complete. The psychometric properties of the SSBS-2 are acceptable. Measures of internal consistency are above .90, and test–retest correlations are generally acceptable, but some correlations were lower than what is considered satisfactory. Criterion validity evidence indicates strong correlations with other similar instruments (Alfonso, Rentz, Orlovsky, & Ramos, 2007). This instrument would not be appropriate as a universal screener because secondary teachers would not have time to complete it for all of their students, and completing it for students who are not presenting concerns is not a judicious use of teacher time. But once teachers have documented concerns about a student (possibly through a teacher nomination process), the SSBS-2 would be a reasonable follow-up instrument to provide a norm-referenced perspective on the degree of problems and the social competencies of the students. Obviously the SSBS-2 is not multigated, but it could be a component in a gated process. Including a means of understanding the social competencies of a student who may be at risk is an especially important component of screening.

Student Risk Screening Scale

The Student Risk Screening Scale (SRSS; Drummond, 1994) is considered a universal screening measure of antisocial or externalizing behaviors; it is not multigated. The one-page measure contains a list of all the students from a teacher's roster or homeroom; teachers are asked to complete seven questions that use a 4-point Likert-type scale. The questions address behaviors such as stealing, lying, cheating, and sneaking. Two questions target some internalizing concerns by asking whether the student has a negative attitude or low achievement. Lane, Kalberg, Parks, and Carter (2008) have used the SRSS in studies and have found its use acceptable. Measures of internal consistency were above .75 in a middle school population, test–retest correlations were significantly strong, and there was evidence of criterion validity (Lane, Parks, Kalberg, & Carter, 2007). This instrument is appealing because teachers can complete the instrument in about 10–15 minutes, gathering information about all of the students in the class. It can be quickly administered and scored; it addresses behaviors that are disruptive and correlate with school failure. However, it does not include sufficient items that would screen for internalizing behaviors.

Behavioral and Emotional Screening System

The Behavioral and Emotional Screening System (BASC-2 BESS; Kamphaus & Reynolds, 2007) is based on the respected Behavior Assessment System for Children, Second Edition (Reynolds & Kamphaus, 2004). The BASC-2 BESS requires about 5 minutes per student for teachers to complete, with additional time for scoring. Although not multigated, it is norm referenced, providing a comparison of risk status. A total of 27 questions are included that address both internalizing and externalizing behaviors. This instrument has high internal consistency (.96–.97), and the test–retest reliability was .91 (Kamphaus & Reynolds).

In typical secondary settings, teachers could complete this measure for each student, but some effort would be misdirected as some students do not need to be included in this level of screening. This instrument may be useful when combined with a teacher nomination process, similar to the first gate of the SSBD, or when combined with a review of other existing data such as ODR or attendance records.

Existing Data

As part of the screening process, school teams should also review ODRs, grades, attendance records, history of in-school and out-of-school suspensions, end-of-year standardized testing, or other commonly kept data. This type of data can be combined with formal screening data to provide a fairly comprehensive summary of students' needs and history without requiring an extensive amount of faculty time. For example, students who have excessive ODRs or even a few consistent ODRs may need opportunities to review their behavior, learn and practice new skills, and make goals for improvement. In our experience, about 5% of the students in a school generate at least 50% of the ODRs. If ODRs are recorded and reviewed, these students could easily be identified and targeted for intervention. Students like Nichole, mentioned in the introductory vignette, would have been identified by reviewing grades and attendance. If students have multiple out-of-school suspensions, the second suspension could trigger a team meeting to proactively work on the problem and determine needed interventions.

Effective screening could be completed by a process that consistently and systematically reviews data. Homeroom teachers or first-period teachers could review grades, attendance, and/ or other data for their students each month. Using predetermined criteria based on local norms, teams could discuss students who appear to have emerging or well-developed problems.

SUMMARY

Screening is an extremely important aspect of implementing a continuum of interventions for students with behavioral and emotional problems. If a continuum of services is developed but there is not a systematic means for matching students to interventions, teams are essentially maintaining the traditional approach of waiting for students to fail before providing services. Without a systematic approach to identify students, delivery of interventions is based on teacher referral, which depends on teacher tolerance levels and expectations that tend to be inconsistent and change over time. Screening facilitates identifying students who need a variety of interventions, which is discussed in Chapters 8 and 9.

CHAPTER 8

Targeted Interventions
Tier 2

With Tier 1 strategies in place and students identified who are less responsive to schoolwide behavior improvement efforts, the planning team at Wesley Junior High is moving forward with Tier 2 interventions. They decide to offer a social skills class in which selected students who have demonstrated ongoing behavior problems in spite of Tier 1 efforts can receive additional instruction and support for elective course credit. Woven into the social skills curriculum, students will be given opportunities to learn goal setting and self-monitoring skills and to be involved in service learning field trips in the community.

The planning team at a middle school in a neighboring community decides to take a different approach. Rather than offer a new course, this team decides to add social skills instruction, individual goal setting, and self-monitoring to an enhanced English course, with only about 15 rather than the usual 25 students in the class. The teacher cooperates with the planning team in selecting literature and activities for the course related to the ongoing behavioral challenges of students identified as needing Tier 2 support. Since all students are required to take English classes, this enhanced curriculum will be made available to students beyond those who have been screened for Tier 2 interventions. However, plans are made for monitoring the progress of the Tier 2 students who participate in these classes and for taking the needs of these students into account when planning instruction.

As explained, Tier 1 strategies are primarily focused on prevention and early intervention. If designed and implemented well these strategies should help to prevent most school behavior problems. At the Tier 2 level, interventions are targeted specifically to the behavior problems exhibited by a smaller percentage of students. Behaviors associated with Tier 2 interventions may be characterized as persistent in spite of Tier 1 efforts: for example, excessive talking out of turn, disruptive behavior, noncompliance, and persistent inattention. Adolescents who have been recommended by their teachers for Tier 2 interventions tend to perform at lower academic levels on average and to have more office referrals as well as more problem behaviors in class than the majority of their peers (Caldarella et al., 2008; Richardson et al., 2009). Thus it is crucial to provide support for students functioning at this level and to move them, if possible, toward Tier 1 functioning.

In this chapter we discuss Tier 2 interventions that planning teams can implement for small groups of students who persistently exhibit troublesome social and academic behaviors. These interventions can be organized into a separate curriculum, as in the example of Wesley Junior High, or considered as part of an integrated curriculum in existing courses. Since a primary goal of Tier 2 interventions is to replace existing problem behaviors with positive behaviors that do not require intervention, a goal of self-management can be considered foundational on this level. A student who is managing his or her own behavior and making appropriate corrections can be considered as functioning within a Tier 1 level. For the most part these students require little or no additional intervention beyond Tier 1 supports. Students who require a teacher or administrator to manage their behavior—more than is required for the majority (e.g., 80–85%) of their peers—are typically functioning at Tier 2 or 3. Accordingly, this chapter first considers the goal of self-management and recommends interventions in light of that goal. That is, interventions in this chapter are considered in terms of an overarching goal of having new positive behaviors become part of a student's own repertoire—as habitual aspects of successful self-management.

> A primary goal of Tier 2 interventions is to replace existing problem behaviors with positive behaviors that do not require intervention.

SELF-MANAGEMENT

The term *self-management*, as used in this chapter, requires that we specify what the *self* is managing. We emphasize the management *by* the student of one or more specific behaviors, thoughts, or emotional responses, rather than the management *of* the student (by self or others). Self-management, from this perspective, means *doing* something adaptive rather than simply *stopping* a behavior, which is often referred to as "self-control." In this sense, self-management is a much more productive request than self-control, considering that stopping a behavior (self-control) may involve aversive consequences, while learning a new behavior (self-management) often involves a reinforcing consequence. A student is much more likely to cooperate for a reward than for a punishment (Young, West, Smith, & Morgan, 1991).

Several components are usually involved in teaching self-management, each including several steps. At least one of these components should involve students as primarily responsible participants—with the goal of increasing student participation in all components. These include assessing needs, establishing behavioral objectives, implementing interventions, and monitoring outcomes (Young et al., 1991). Each of these components is addressed in turn.

Assessing Needs

The previous chapter discussed the importance of accurate screening in identifying students who need additional support. Identification is just the first step in assessing needs. The nature of required support must be decided after a close examination of the academic, behavioral, social, and emotional expectations in the school environment, an assessment of where selected students are in relation to these expectations, and a determination of where to begin closing the gaps.

Behavior, both of students and adults, is typically sandwiched between antecedents and consequences. Often behavior is initially prompted by a situation or environment, with consequences that increase or decrease the likelihood that the behavior is repeated. When applied to teaching students to assess and manage their own behaviors, this sequence has been referred to as the ABCs of self-management (e.g., Young et al., 1991).

The ABCs for Tier 2 interventions typically focus on assessing patterns of antecedents, behaviors, and consequences for selected students as a group rather than individually. For example, observing that identified students receive the most ODRs for violating lunchroom rules begins to address all of the ABCs: something is known about (1) the antecedent situation (lunchtime), (2) the nature of the behavior (the most common rule violation), and (3) the consequences (an ODR). Thus the need to improve student behavior during lunchtime has been identified, and the ABCs supporting the current situation are apparent. At this point more detail about the interactions should be obtained:

> **Behavior, both of students and adults, is typically sandwiched between antecedents and consequences.**

- What aspects of the lunchroom environment might have contributed to the behavior?
- Did students understand the expectations and consequences?
- Were there other, perhaps unintended, consequences (e.g., attention from peers and adults, time away from class)?

To better understand the antecedents and consequences contributing to behavior, students can be involved in the assessment stage and encouraged to share their perspectives. While the adults might suggest more supervision, students might point out unclear expectations for lunchroom behavior (e.g., "We didn't know we were breaking a rule until we were sent to the office"). Or students might point out lack of incentives for behaving appropriately and minimal impact of current consequences. By sharing in the assessment process, students can learn not only to assess their own behaviors, experiences, and needs, but also to understand more about the process of changing their own behaviors, which could lead to better self-management. A discussion with students about these ABCs may produce a more complete picture, as student perceptions will likely differ from adult perceptions, and students are more likely to feel some engagement and ownership of the process, as well as more autonomy.

Establishing Behavioral Objectives

After a more specific assessment of needs, the team needs to clearly define the sort of change that would be beneficial for everyone involved. With the lunchroom ODRs, the staff members referring students to the office see the behavior problems, and administrators likely see problems as well. At this point staff members and administrators need to address how they would like to see students behave (e.g., putting trash away instead of throwing it, waiting in line instead of cutting in) and possibly solicit student perspectives (e.g., desire for more opportunities to eat outside the lunchroom). Allowing students to eat outside the lunchroom contingent on their picking up trash and maintaining orderly lines could link the objectives of both adults and students.

> **Students and adults should remember that eliminating a problem behavior is usually only half of the solution.**

Students and adults should remember that eliminating a problem behavior is usually only half of the solution. Teaching an alternative behavior with more positive consequences should be emphasized in efforts to stop inappropriate behaviors. Both groups also need to address the purpose or function of past behaviors and select new behaviors that might serve those purposes better. For example, if students have misbehaved in order to break school monotony, have fun, or to gain peer attention, they can learn more effective behaviors to accomplish the same purposes (e.g., appropriately beginning a conversation or effectively organizing an activity).

> **As students, administrators, and staff members discuss the prevalent ABCs, ideas should emerge for working together for a better situation.**

As students, administrators, and staff members discuss the prevalent ABCs, ideas should emerge for working together for a better situation. Staff and administrators might be able to change antecedents, such as allowing students to eat outside the lunchroom, allowing organized lunchtime activities, or increasing supervision in the lunchroom. They might also find a need to change consequences, providing incentives for positive behaviors along with office referrals for undesirable behaviors. As in other phases, involving secondary school students in establishing objectives is developmentally appropriate for encouraging self-management for adolescents because they tend to show reasonable problem-solving skills and abstract thinking.

Implementing Interventions

As the most effective interventions involve both reducing undesirable behaviors and increasing desirable alternatives, we explore in this section some interventions designed to increase behaviors that improve both social and academic outcomes, including

- Social skills instruction.
- Goal setting.
- Social and emotional learning.
- Service learning.
- Mentoring.
- Administrator teaching in response to ODRs.

Each of these interventions is discussed in more detail below.

Social Skills Instruction

As addressed in Chapter 5, most efforts at improving behavior in secondary schools will be enhanced by emphasis on specific social skills instruction, particularly with students at Tiers 2 and 3 where general instruction, reminders, and incentives at the schoolwide level do not affect behavior sufficiently.

At the Tier 2 level, social skills instruction should take into account not only the skills identified as schoolwide expectations but also social skills linked to particular needs identified during screening and assessment. As noted in Chapter 7, behavioral difficulties can often be categorized as *externalizing*, those directed outward (e.g., talking out of turn, act-

> **Social skills instruction should take into account not only the skills identified as schoolwide expectations but also social skills linked to particular needs identified during screening and assessment.**

ing aggressively, arguing), and *internalizing*, those directed inward (e.g., social withdrawal, flat affect, low activity levels). Social skills that address internalizing behaviors might include greeting others, making conversation, asking and answering questions, expressing feelings, and so on. Social skills that address externalizing behaviors might include accepting consequences, following directions, coping with conflict, and appropriately expressing feelings (see Goldstein, 1999; Goldstein & McGinnis, 1997; Merrell & Gimpel, 1998, for additional examples and steps for teaching).

When organizing Tier 2 instruction according to student needs, school personnel must consider the potential for social support or negative labeling that might occur in different group compositions. For example, the junior high mentioned at the beginning of the chapter designed a specific social skills class for students identified by the teachers as needing extra support. The separate class provided a focused intervention, but some students felt that they were being targeted as "problem students" and would be labeled as such by their peers because they were in the class. At the middle school the enhanced English course included students who were functioning at all tiers, thus eliminating the risk of labeling and increasing social support from a wider peer group; however, a less focused intervention might have resulted.

Organizing a group consisting solely of students identified for specific behavioral concerns (e.g., externalizing or internalizing) could cause an initial escalation of negative behaviors, with similar problems being compounded by proximity. In addition to providing wider social support, broadening the group might result in better generalization of skills (practicing them with a wider variety of peers). Instruction in such mixed groups may necessarily become less focused on specific needs, but better able to address overlapping needs: for example, skills such as socialization might benefit both internalizing and externalizing students though perhaps for different reasons. Merrell and Gimpel (1998) provide a detailed discussion of these and other issues in designing group social skills interventions.

Other significant considerations for Tier 2 interventions are planning for generalization and tracking behavior over time and across settings. Since Tier 2 students have not responded adequately to Tier 1 social skills instruction, they may require closer observation and more opportunities to generalize the skills, even if the skill set doesn't change dramatically between tiers. Tracking behavior is an intervention that can promote generalization and maintenance of behavior. Tracking behavior in various settings and at different times encourages generalization because students monitor their own behavior. Thus, involving students in tracking their own use of the social skills not only encourages generalization, but also encourages self-management, as well as allowing for a point of comparison with other measures (e.g., teacher and parent reports) (Peterson, Young, Salzberg, & West, 2006). For example, students might track their behavior in a daily log, noting times they practiced a social skill in or out of the class. These self-reports could be "signed off" by teachers, parents, or administrators, or can be compared with independent observations by others. Other ideas for encouraging generalization include the following (see Goldstein & McGinnis, 1997; Merrell & Gimpel, 1998):

- Overlearning (practice, practice, practice).
- Varying models, participants (e.g., different role-play pairings), times, and settings.
- Varying reinforcers (e.g., praise, positive note to parents, prizes, pizza party for the group).
- Varying reinforcement schedules (e.g., continuous to partial reinforcement using a variable ratio schedule).
- Fading prompts (reminding the students less often to use social skills as the skills are acquired).
- Moving toward natural reinforcers (e.g., peer praise), and natural environments (e.g., encouraging skill use in regular classrooms, hallways, lunchroom, and nonschool settings).
- Shifting responsibility for training and practice to students (self-management).

Goal Setting

> From learning social skills and other behaviors to academic achievement, goal setting should be a central aspect of all improvement efforts with students.

From learning social skills and other behaviors to academic achievement, goal setting should be a central aspect of all improvement efforts with students—especially those aimed at increasing self-management. Like Lewis Carroll's Alice in Wonderland, if we don't know where we want to go, it doesn't much matter which direction we take. Effective goal setting includes several components (Merrell, 2007a, 2007b):

1. Defining values.
2. Aligning goals with values.
3. Outlining the steps and resources necessary to reach goals.
4. Evaluating whether goals are reasonably attainable.
5. Developing a timeline and building in accountability.
6. Evaluating progress.

In Tier 2 interventions, educators should particularly attend to how Tier 2 goals align both with student goals and Tier 1 goals. Where goals overlap, educators and students are likely to find shared values that can inform multiple goals. For example, efforts at Tier 1 and 2 might share the value of creating safe, nurturing environments. This value may be approached differently from the different tiers, such as setting a Tier 1 goal to increase teacher writing of praise notes for all students, and setting a Tier 2 goal of increasing positive peer interactions among students who have multiple ODRs involving peer conflicts. These goals may also be aligned with a student goal of receiving more positive feedback from teachers or peers.

Planning teams must also ensure that goals are specific and reasonably attainable. The importance of reasonably attainable goals can be illustrated by a contrast among goals to "work harder," "complete more assignments," and "get the highest score in class." The goal to work harder is certainly attainable, but it is difficult to define and measure. Achieving the highest score in the class depends in part on the performance of others, and clearly not everyone can achieve this goal. However, the goal to complete more assignments is definable, measurable, and attainable by the student, independent of the performance of other students. This goal could be further specified as "completing three more assignments each week" or "completing at least 85% of assignments," which also indicates the type of measurement needed along with the specific goal.

Successfully reaching goals, like successfully learning social skills, sometimes requires breaking down more complex goals into specific steps. Outlining the steps to completing a goal can also help in assessing whether the goal is reasonably attainable. For example, turning in a higher percentage of homework might involve (1) gathering a list of upcoming assignments, (2) creating a study schedule, (3) organizing notebooks and folders, and (4) tracking assignment completion. Each of these steps is attainable and measurable, whereas a goal to get an "A" in every class might not always lend itself to clearly attainable and measurable steps—especially since some grading procedures may emphasize performance relative to other students or to established norms, other procedures might emphasize individual effort, and still others the mastery of various skills across time.

Once goals are set and the steps outlined for attaining them, students and educators may both benefit from creating reasonable time lines with opportunities for recording and reporting progress along the way. The time line will, of course, vary according to the goal set and the needs of the students. The goal and time line of initiating one conversation by the end of the week might be a monumental task for a very timid student, but a relatively meaningless task for a student who frequently creates disruptions by talking in class.

Finally, efforts are more likely to be maintained if accountability is built into the process. Students can report to friends or classmates, teachers, parents, and so on. Such reports are more likely to be beneficial if they assess progress along the way, giving an opportunity for correction rather than simply assessing success or failure at the goal deadline. Setting goals and assessing progress are crucial in learning self-management. Form 8.1 (at the end of the chapter) is an example of a goal chart that could be used for this purpose; Figure 8.1 illustrates a completed goal chart.

Goal: Be on time to class at least 95% of the time

When? Assessed at the end of 2 weeks

   Step 1: Create a graph or chart to track daily progress

   When? 2nd period today

   Step 2: Tell friends about my goal so they will understand when I limit time talking between classes

   When? Between classes today

   Step 3: Check in with mentor/teacher to report progress

   When? Daily

   Step4: Buy or borrow an alarm clock, or request a wake-up call

   When? By the end of the day

FIGURE 8.1. Example of a completed goal chart.

Social and Emotional Learning

Resilience has been described "both as an outcome of adaptation and as a process of adaptation" (Olsson, Bond, Burns, Vella-Brodrick, & Sawyer, 2003, p. 9). The secondary school years are in many ways synonymous with change. As noted in Chapter 2, bodies are changing, relationships are changing, thinking patterns are changing, identities are changing, and expectations (both of self and others) are changing. Adapting emotionally to these changes is not always easy, but some students seem to have a much easier time than others. Several skills have been identified that support emotional resilience, including the following (Merrell, 2007a, 2007b):

1. The ability to understand one's own emotions.
2. The ability to understand the emotions of others.
3. The ability to appropriately regulate negative emotions and stress.
4. The ability to identify and correct thinking errors.
5. Problem-solving and conflict resolution skills.
6. The ability to cultivate optimism.

> **Teaching emotional resilience, rather than simply assuming that students either have it or don't have it, suggests that students who struggle with emotional regulation can learn to increase self-management of the skills associated with resilience.**

One approach to teaching these skills, which can be adapted both for preventative efforts at Tier 1 and intervention efforts at Tiers 2 and 3, can be found in Merrell's *Strong Kids* (2007a) or *Strong Teens* (2007b) curriculum. This approach has been used effectively at Tier 2 in order to address internalizing concerns, which are otherwise often neglected (Marchant, Brown, Caldarella, & Young, 2010).

Teaching emotional resilience, rather than simply assuming that students either have it or don't have it, suggests that students who struggle with emotional regulation can learn to increase self-management of the skills associated with resilience.

Service Learning

Opportunities to provide service to others at school or in the community can help students gain and practice social and emotional skills in real-world settings, rather than being limited to traditional classroom instruction. There are many benefits associated with service learning (see, e.g., McGuire & Gamble, 2006; Steinberg, 2008; Stott & Jackson, 2005; Yates & Youniss, 1996):

- Personal awareness.
- Social skills.
- Learning skills.
- Career interests.
- Character education.
- Moral identity.
- Social responsibility.
- Community belonging.
- Self-esteem and efficacy.

- Academic skills.
- Improved mental health.
- Decreased problem behavior.

To facilitate these benefits, service learning should be aligned to the desired specific outcomes. For example, if teachers/administrators hope that service learning will improve student–teacher relationships, then teachers and students should work together in ways that provide opportunities for positive interactions. If they intend for service learning to increase a certain social skill, such as starting a conversation, they should design service-learning opportunities that will cause students to use that skill in different settings. For example, taking students to serve at a homeless shelter with teachers simply overseeing their efforts might not improve relationships between teachers and students, but could help students practice the skill of starting a conversation and improve generalization of this skill outside the classroom. If, on the other hand, teachers work side-by-side with students in such service, both goals might be facilitated.

> **Service learning should be aligned to the desired specific outcomes.**

Other important aspects of successful service-learning experiences include psychological engagement (McGuire & Gamble, 2006) and time for reflection about the service and lessons learned from it (Steinberg, 2008). Several websites are dedicated to providing service-learning information and opportunities; a few of these follow:

- *www.servicelearning.org*
- *www.service-learningpartnership.org*
- *www.nylc.org*

Although numerous opportunities for service learning are available in communities, service learning need not always require time away from school. Service learning can include mentoring or tutoring younger students or even simply using talents and expertise to enrich the education of classmates. When students participate in selecting and planning or even seeking and initiating their own service-learning opportunities, self-management skills can be further expanded.

Mentoring

Just as caring for and assisting others can improve adolescents' social and emotional well-being, being assisted by a caring mentor can make a crucial difference in a secondary school student's own success. Having at least one caring adult in a student's life is considered a crucial factor in facilitating success academically, behaviorally, and socially (e.g., Dappen & Isernhagen, 2005). The individualized nature of mentoring makes it a potentially effective Tier 3 intervention, as we discuss in Chapter 9. However, mentoring has been shown to be effective as a Tier 2 intervention as well (Caldarella, Adams, Valentine, & Young, 2009). One reason mentoring can be particularly beneficial, as well as efficient, at Tier 2 is that mentors from the community can potentially have

> **Having at least one caring adult in a student's life is considered a crucial factor in facilitating success academically, behaviorally, and socially.**

a great impact on students at this tier before more extensive Tier 3 concerns emerge that would require more extensive mentor training and expertise.

To be successful, mentoring programs require careful planning. Planning teams should identify the specific goals of the program, obtain or develop outcome measures that are directly linked to the program goals, and seek support in the school and in the wider community sufficient to sustain the program. Several additional recommendations have been made in planning and implementing successful mentoring programs (Dappen & Isernhagen, 2005):

- Mentoring programs should center on developing caring relationships and building trust. Students should be confident that the mentor has their best interests in mind and is capable of supporting and guiding them toward achieving their goals.
- Parents and students should be informed of (1) program goals and measures, (2) potential risks and benefits, and (3) qualifications for participation of mentors as well as students.
- Potential pools for recruiting mentors may include school staff, peers, parents, and volunteers from the community. Community leaders, service organizations, businesses, and retirement centers are often good sources for potential mentors.
- In finding mentors, particular consideration should be given to the willingness and ability of a mentor to make a fairly long-term commitment to the mentoring relationship (preferably more than 6 months).
- Mentors should be able to attend whatever training may be related to the specific aims of the program. Training may include instruction on program goals and methods, school policies and procedures, and effective practices for working with youth. Usually mentoring also requires some type of background check for the sake of student safety.
- Administrators might want to consider matching mentors with students according to interests, needs, personality, or expertise.

Although mentoring opportunities are most effective when they are long term, they are rarely permanent. Thus mentoring opportunities should focus on encouraging self-management and goal setting in the other areas previously discussed. Mentoring opportunities might also involve helping students learn to seek and appropriately solicit additional mentoring as needed (e.g., from parents, educators, other students, older siblings, neighbors), as well as encouraging them to become mentors for others.

Administrative Interventions

Occasionally, in spite of other Tier 2 interventions, students will need to be referred to the office for additional teaching from administrators. Sometimes ODRs may even increase initially when SWPBS is implemented, as teachers and other school staff begin to attend more closely to student behaviors at Tier 2 and work to correct them. However, administrator teaching (not simply punishing) can be a powerful tool in improving student behavior and ultimately reducing ODRs.

As a reminder (see Chapter 5), administrative teaching applies across the three tiers, but teaching in response to an ODR is more representative of interventions at Tiers 2 and 3. Specifically, at Tier 1 the guidelines for ODRs are communicated to teachers and students primarily as a preventive measure. Students functioning at a Tier 1 level might occasionally be referred for office discipline, a one-on-one teaching opportunity, but these behaviors and referrals would generally be relatively minor or atypical for the student. Tier 2 administrative interventions are typically in response to either ongoing behavioral problems or serious infractions. Administrator involvement in Tier 3 interventions is discussed further in Chapter 9. Beyond the typical teaching response, these interventions might include behavior contracting, regular tracking of behavioral progress, and increased parental involvement.

When a teacher has determined that an ODR is necessary and a student is sent to the office, the following steps are a general sequence for an effective administrative response (see Black & Downs, 1993):

1. Administrator assesses whether the student is willing to follow basic instructions, such as "Please sit down." If the student is noncompliant, the administrator begins an "intensive teaching" interaction. (See "Intensive Teaching" below.)
2. If the student is generally compliant to the administrator's initial instructions, the administrator checks with the teacher to get a specific description of the problem behavior and determine an alternative behavior for the teaching interaction.
3. The administrator returns to the student and again assesses the student's compliance with basic instructions. Specific details of the student's behavior, such as the student's posture, facial expressions, and so on, can help in assessing compliance.
4. When the student is following simple instructions, the administrator can begin a teaching interaction focused on teaching an appropriate alternative to the problem behavior. (See "Corrective Teaching" below.)
5. When the student has successfully rehearsed and demonstrated the new behavior, the administrator checks again with the teacher to prepare him or her to accept an apology from the student.
6. The administrator returns to the student and teaches/rehearses an appropriate apology and commitment the student can make.
7. The student gives the apology and commitment to the teacher and, if appropriate, the student is admitted back into the class.

For the administrative intervention to be most effective, conditions for the student to return to the class should be clearly outlined with the teacher. For example, the administrator and teacher might discuss what constitutes a sincere and acceptable apology. Students might also be expected to make a specific commitment to use the new behavior in place of the old problem behavior if they are to return to class. Depending on the frequency or severity of the problem behavior, this commitment might involve a written agreement (i.e., behavior contract), with specific consequences for compliance and noncompliance agreed upon and signed by the student, teacher, administrator, and in some cases a parent.

INTENSIVE TEACHING

When a student is noncompliant with an administrator's instructions, the administrator should seek compliance before moving on to additional teaching. It is important, through each of the steps below, that the administrator models the behavior he or she is requesting of the student. For example, if the administrator expects the student to use a calm voice, the administrator should use a calm voice. The steps of this process are outlined below:

1. Give a brief expression of empathy or praise (e.g., "I can see that you might be upset; thank you for staying in the office").
2. Briefly describe the problem behavior currently being exhibited by the student (e.g., "You are pacing and shouting").
3. Briefly give a clear and specific instruction and meaningful rationale to correct the current problem behavior (e.g., "You need to sit down and lower your voice so that we can resolve this issue").
4. Give the student time to comply, and praise approximations to the instruction. For example, if the student lowers her or his voice, the administrator might say, "Thank you for lowering your voice, now please take a seat."
5. If the student remains noncompliant, repeat the steps of the intensive teaching intervention. Do not continue the overall administrative response until the student is generally compliant. Additional teaching will be less effective if the student is not listening and responding.

CORRECTIVE TEACHING

Corrective teaching is similar to intensive teaching. However, intensive teaching focuses on immediate "out-of-control" behavior in the office, and on achieving instructional control—or getting the student to follow basic instructions. Corrective teaching addresses a past behavior (i.e., the behavior for which the student was sent to the office) and on teaching an appropriate alternative. As with intensive teaching, the administrator should always model the appropriate behavior she or he intends to teach.

1. Begin with a brief expression of praise or empathy (e.g., "I understand that you were frustrated" or "I appreciate that you waited here quietly for me").
2. Briefly describe the problem behavior (e.g., "When your teacher asked you to take your seat, you refused and swore").
3. Briefly and clearly describe the alternative behavior (e.g., "What you need to do when given an instruction by your teacher is (a) look at the teacher, (b) say "OK," and (c) follow the instruction).
4. Give a brief but meaningful rationale for using the alternative behavior (e.g., "Following instructions at the right time will show respect, and in turn you will be respected").
5. Demonstrate the new behavior with a role play.
6. Give the student an opportunity to practice.
7. Praise the student's efforts and repeat the practice until the student demonstrates mastery.

As noted in previous chapters, an advantage of a teaching approach to discipline over simply imposing a consequence (such as in-school or out-of-school suspension, a call home, loss of privileges, etc.) is that in such a teaching interaction the student is provided the tools to avoid problem behaviors in the future. Through each stage of the administrative intervention, the focus should be on teaching appropriate alternatives to the problem behavior or on preparing the student to receive such instruction. These teaching interactions can be used effectively by teachers as well as by administrators.

> **Through each stage of the administrative intervention, the focus should be on teaching appropriate alternatives to the problem behavior or on preparing the student to receive such instruction.**

Monitoring Outcomes

Outcome measures for Tier 2 interventions may include a second look at the behaviors that resulted in students being placed at the Tier 2 level. For example, for students who were initially selected for Tier 2 interventions because of excessive ODRs, one outcome measure should be a decrease in referrals and an increase in use of a new appropriate skill. Other outcome measures can include grades in a specific class, number of assignments turned in with 80% accuracy, behavioral observations from teachers and other staff members, parent reports, and student self-reports.

It is crucial that whatever measures are selected are aligned to the specific goals of an intervention, as well as to more general goals such as decreasing problem behaviors in the school. For example, if a goal-setting intervention aims at increasing the number of completed homework assignments, the best outcome measure would be the number of assignments completed before and after the intervention rather than an overall grade at the end of the course. Similarly, the most direct measure of a social skill intervention would be observations of the extent to which students exhibit that particular social skill before and after the intervention. The increased performance of a given skill may not be detectable in a global measure of social functioning (e.g., from a comprehensive social skills questionnaire), unless other contributions to global social functioning are included in the intervention being assessed. A complete outcome assessment might thus require both specific and more global measures. Examining both specific and global measures can help identify where the gaps between present and desired functioning have been closed and where gaps remain.

Global measures of improved behavior at Tier 2 often include the number of ODRs, course grades, or test scores. Specific measures are limited primarily by the type of intervention employed in a given setting. In lunchroom misbehavior, for example, one measure of specific improvement might be less trash collected from the lunchroom tables and floors after lunch. For a more complete assessment of the outcome of lunchtime intervention, behavioral observations might be tracked across time, along with the number and type of ODRs occurring during lunchtime.

In keeping with our emphasis on replacing negative behaviors with more positive alternatives, measures of increases in desirable behaviors might be added to the often more typical measures of undesirable behaviors. So in the example of lunchroom misbehavior, outcome measures might not only track a decrease in shoving in the lunch line and a decrease in clutter, but might also look for increased invitations for another person to go first in line and increased cleanup efforts. Attending to an increase in positive behaviors not only adds important outcome measures but allows these behaviors to be more readily rewarded.

SUMMARY

In this chapter we have discussed Tier 2 interventions in the context of teaching self-management and involving students in the processes of assessing needs, establishing behavioral objectives, implementing interventions, and monitoring outcomes. We discussed several interventions that might be adapted for Tier 2 instruction and supports: social skills instruction, goal setting, social and emotional learning, service learning, mentoring, and administrative interventions. As part of administrative interventions, we described intensive and corrective teaching as procedures for helping students comply with instructions as well as learn and practice new behaviors. These teaching procedures can be useful for teachers and other school personnel as well. In the next chapter we describe Tier 3 interventions for students who continue to exhibit behavior problems even with Tier 2 interventions and supports.

Goal Chart

Goal: _____

_____

When? _____

_____

Step 1: _____

When? _____

Step 2: _____

When? _____

Step 3: _____

When? _____

Step4: _____

When? _____

CHAPTER 9

Individual Interventions
Tier 3

Cindy was brought to the attention of her junior high school planning team after being identified by schoolwide screening as a potential participant in Tier 2 interventions. She was included in an enhanced English course, which was designed to link language instruction to social skills development. While most students in the class responded well to the additional social skills instruction and classwide reinforcement for positive behavior, Cindy's behavior problems continued and even seemed to intensify. She was frequently sent to the office for behaviors that included making sexual comments and gestures, throwing books, pencils, and other objects, and failing to complete her work. Cindy's office visits became so frequent that in order to avoid interfering with her educational progress, a staff member was assigned to provide one-on-one instruction and tutoring in a private room adjoining the office. A few of Cindy's teachers learned to preempt Cindy's problem behavior by having her report voluntarily to the office if she was having a "bad day."

However, whenever Cindy returned to her classes, her problematic behaviors also returned—and the amount of disruption she created seemed to be increasing over time. No interventions appeared to help Cindy productively engage in learning activities. Cindy's English teacher began to suspect that Cindy's behavior was enabling her either to escape interaction with peers in the classroom or to gain more one-on-one adult attention. In order to explore these possibilities, the planning team decided that more in-depth, individualized information gathering and problem solving were warranted in order to find ways to help Cindy to participate in her classes.

As suggested by Cindy's experience, Tier 3 interventions are needed to resolve problem behaviors for individual students when Tier 1 and Tier 2 efforts have failed to effect sufficient positive change. Tier 3 interventions are appropriate for persistent externalizing or internalizing behaviors. Some of these behaviors may threaten a student's well-being or the well-being of other students in a classroom, and other behaviors may be disruptive or tend to isolate the student. Behaviors associated with Tier 3 may sometimes require referrals to mental health professionals or programs outside of the school, which are discussed later in this chapter. However, there is much that educators can do in order to ameliorate or even resolve behavior problems that require a more focused, individualized response, possibly enabling students with significant difficult behaviors to continue to participate in mainstream classrooms and helping them move toward functioning well with Tier 1 or 2 supports.

Tier 3 interventions are not drastically different from Tier 2 interventions. The most notable differences are (1) the intensity or "dosage" of the services required to facilitate positive change, and (2) often an individual rather than small-group focus of the interventions. Some students may need individualized interventions because of severe learning and behavioral deficits. Others served in Tier 3 may have an extensive history of educational failure; their needs may have exhausted the resources of previous settings, and earlier interventions may not have targeted key behaviors. Although a primary goal of Tier 3 interventions is to move students toward success with Tier 1 or 2 supports, some students may need long-term Tier 3 supports because of their unique needs or circumstances.

When Tier 1 and Tier 2 efforts have failed to effect change in an individual student's behavior, more or different interventions are needed. This is not necessarily because the Tier 1 and 2 efforts were ineffective, but because interventions in these tiers are typically designed for groups. Sometimes students have behaviors, emotions, and needs that are beyond the resources and capacity of these interventions. In effect, a student may need a higher or different intervention "dose." If the majority of students (but not all) respond well to Tier 1 and 2 strategies, these interventions probably do not need amending. However, understanding and targeting the needs and circumstances of students with significantly challenging behaviors—through drawing on meaningful data—is the focus for Tier 3. This requires a more in-depth examination of the student's behaviors and the contexts in which behaviors are exhibited. In the next section we provide an overview of the problem-solving process for facilitating targeted interventions at Tier 3. We then describe two tools for implementing this process at Tier 3: functional behavioral assessments and behavior intervention plans.

THE PROBLEM-SOLVING PROCESS

The problem-solving process first described in Chapter 6 provides a framework for making accurate, targeted, and data-based decisions about what is needed in interventions at all three tiers. If a problem-solving approach is implemented only at Tier 3, interventions and strategies at the other tiers may not be targeting

> **The problem-solving process provides a framework for making accurate, targeted, and data-based decisions about what is needed in interventions at all three tiers.**

the heart of the problems or addressing the solutions that are most likely to result in positive change with the fewest resources. Teams should be familiar with using the problem-solving process as it applies to systems (Tier 1), small groups (Tier 2), and specific academic or behavioral concerns for *individual students* (Tier 3). As efforts at each tier are most likely to be effective when linked to efforts at the other tiers, effective Tier 3 interventions depend on using the problem-solving process across all the tiers of the system (Burns & Gibbons, 2008).

The following steps are commonly included in the problem-solving process (Florida Department of Education, 2006):

1. *Problem identification.* The problem is described in observable, behavioral terms. Reasons *why* the problem or problems are occurring are identified.
2. *Plan development.* An individualized plan is developed that is based on the data collected from other intervention outcomes and additional data that may be needed.
3. *Plan implementation.* The plan is carried out and progress toward goals is monitored. The integrity of the implementation is also included in the data that are collected at this stage.
4. *Evaluation.* Data are examined to determine whether the plan is working. If modifications are needed, the process begins again with problem identification.

Problem Identification

For Tier 3 interventions, the problem-solving process often involves an FBA and an accompanying behavior intervention plan (BIP). An FBA is a systematic way to determine the purpose of a student's problem (or target) behavior and recognize the events that predict that behavior. FBAs have several components, and it is beyond the scope of this chapter to cover the topic in its entirety. Completing an FBA can also be a challenging task. It is a skill that develops over time and requires collaboration and feedback. Teachers should not attempt to complete FBA observations while they are engaged in their normal teaching activities; rather, assistance should be provided so that observations can be focused. We focus on some of the core features of an FBA and (in the following section) the accompanying BIP. For additional information, Umbreit, Ferro, Liaupsin, and Lane (2007) have written an excellent text on these topics.

The first step in conducting an FBA is to correctly identify the problematic target behavior. This task is often more difficult than it may appear. The difficulty frequently lies in the fact that teachers, parents, or others may use general terms such as *unmotivated* or *disrespectful* when describing a problem behavior. While such descriptions might give a general sense of the problem, they may lead to a sense of frustration because nonspecific problems typically do not evoke specific solutions. They can also result in more time being spent discussing how awful the problem is rather than succinctly identifying the problem and developing solutions. In order for an FBA to be effective, the behavior must be clearly defined, observable, and measurable. "Sarah is often depressed" is not an easily measured behavior, nor does it necessarily suggest a clear solution. However, "Sarah frequently eats lunch by herself" is observable and measureable, and the observation hints at possible solutions (e.g., increasing social opportunities and social competence).

Another error is focusing solely on the outcomes of the target behavior (e.g., "Seth is often sent to the office") rather than the specific behavior that caused the outcome (e.g., "Seth often fights with peers at lunch or during transitions between classes"). As we discussed, identifying the outcomes of behavior is important in fully identifying the problem; however, it is important to distinguish between a target behavior and its *outcomes* or *consequences*.

The next step is identifying a replacement behavior. Such a behavior should be stated in terms of what we want the student to do, rather than simply what we want the individual to stop doing. For example, rather than "decrease her depression," we may want Sarah to "initiate interaction with one peer during lunch." The replacement behavior also should be something the student has, or can gain, the skills to perform. This may involve determining whether the target is a "can't do" or "won't do" problem. Does the student have the emotional and behavioral skills to meet the expectations of the environment? If not, the student needs opportunities for learning and practicing specific skills. When Lilly begins to cry each time she receives a grade that is below her expectations, she may not have the skills to cope with excessive self-criticism (or external criticism). Teaching her how to realistically assess and reframe common thinking errors could be a valuable skill (Merrell, 2007a, 2007b).

On the other hand, if the student knows the skill but the environment punishes or fails to reinforce the appropriate use of that skill, the consequences and environment need to be restructured. Jamie may know how to positively respond when a teacher redirects his horseplay in the lunchroom, but in the classroom when the English teacher asks him to be quiet he explodes and calls the teacher disrespectful names, which results in a visit to the principal's office and thus avoidance of difficult assignments in the class. Replacement behaviors should be supported by the student's natural learning environment. It makes little sense to teach Jamie to raise his hand to ask questions in class if the teacher is going to call on peers who shout out instead.

> **Replacement behaviors should be supported by the student's natural learning environment.**

Correctly identifying target and replacement behaviors requires a variety of assessment strategies. The most common is an interview conducted with teachers and school personnel and, when appropriate, with parent(s) and the student. FBA interviews are often semistructured, with the goals of clearly identifying the target behavior and the conditions under which the behavior occurs (Kern, Dunlap, Clarke, & Childs, 1994; O'Neill, Horner, Albin, Storey, & Sprague, 1997). Form 9.1 (at the end of the chapter) is a basic sample form for conducting an FBA interview and includes some of the typical questions asked in such interviews. Other questions could be added as needed (e.g., Umbreit et al., 2007).

Another strategy for gathering information that is helpful in the FBA process is direct observation using the ABC method. The antecedent (A) refers to the typical conditions (e.g., circumstances or situations) under which behavior (B) occurs, while the consequence (C) is what happens after the behavior, which affects the future occurrence of the behavior. For example, when James is in the lunch line at school he often pushes and shoves his peers. The antecedent is James being in the lunch line. The consequence is that his peers allow James to move to the front of the lunch line when he approaches (i.e., positive reinforcement for pushing). Whereas ABC information can be solicited using interviews, direct observations are often more effective, as data are gathered in real-life settings rather than relying on participants' memories of such events. Direct observations should take place when the target behavior is most likely to occur and be completed by an observer who is in a position to clearly see and hear, but not influence, the target behavior. Interview data can help determine observation times and contexts of observations. Some basic information to record when conducting such observations includes the following:

> **Direct observations should take place when the target behavior is most likely to occur and be completed by an observer who is in a position to clearly see and hear, but not influence, the target behavior.**

- Date, time, and location of the observation.
- Context of the observation (e.g., during class discussions or individual work).

- Student's and observer's names.
- Specific occurrences of the target behavior, antecedents, and consequences (see Figure 9.1).

It is best to continue collecting such information until a consistent pattern of results can be identified. Knowing the patterns will help the problem-solving team generate hypotheses about the function of the target behavior so they can develop interventions.

Behavior generally has two main functions: to get something (positive reinforcement) or to avoid or escape something (negative reinforcement). Umbreit et al. (2007) divide reinforcers into three main categories: attention, tangibles or activities, and sensory reinforcement. These authors further propose a simple 2×3 function matrix that can be helpful in identifying whether the function is positive or negative reinforcement, as well as which of the three categories of reinforcers are maintaining the target behavior. For example, if Sarah often eats by herself at lunch, the team might use interview and direct observation data to answer the following questions:

1. Is Sarah being positively reinforced with attention from others for her behavior?
2. Is she able to avoid attention by eating by herself?
3. Is Sarah being positively reinforced with tangibles or activities when she eats by herself?
4. Is she able to avoid some tangible or activity?
5. Is Sarah receiving some type of positive sensory stimulation?
6. Is she avoiding some sort of sensory stimulation?

Using interview and direct observation data to answer such questions clarifies the function or purpose of Sarah's target behavior. In some situations a behavior may serve multiple functions.

Student: Sarah		Date: Nov. 14	
Observer: Ms. Moreno		Location: Lunchroom	Time: 11:40

Antecedent	Behavior	Consequence
The lunchroom is crowded, most tables are full, several are only partially filled, and one is empty.	Sarah is holding her tray, walking between tables, and looking around the lunchroom.	A female student looks up and moves a backpack making more room at her table as Sarah approaches.
A male student makes eye contact with Sarah and smiles.	Sarah averts her eyes, walks to the empty table, sits down and begins eating.	A female student approaches and sits across from Sarah in one of the vacant seats at her table.
The student sitting across from Sarah says "Hi."	Sarah does not respond, and keeps her head down.	The other student moves to another table.

FIGURE 9.1. Sample ABC observation.

Perhaps Sarah not only avoids contact with her peers (from whom she feels anxiety), but also receives positive attention (expressions of concern) from adults. Such information regarding function is essential to developing appropriate interventions.

Plan Development and Implementation

Once the FBA process is completed, the next step is to design an individualized BIP. Such interventions can be divided into three main categories: teaching replacement behaviors, improving the environment, and adjusting the contingencies (Umbreit et al., 2007). The team may arrange for a student to be taught the skills needed to appropriately meet his or her needs or to serve the function of the target behavior: for example, Sarah might be taught social skills such as how to appropriately enter an ongoing peer activity at lunch. When the environment is improved, positive reinforcement is more easily available for the appropriate replacement behavior: for example, the teacher might make it a habit to praise students for appropriate lunchroom behavior and thus praise Sarah (privately) when she does interact with peers at lunch. Adjusting contingencies can often eliminate the consequence that formerly maintained the target behavior (e.g., asking the teachers to avoid giving attention to Sarah if she eats by herself at lunch).

As suggested previously, before deciding on which intervention strategy or combination of strategies to use, the team must evaluate whether the student is capable of successfully performing the replacement behavior. If the answer is no, then teaching the replacement behavior should be the focus—although the influence of antecedents and consequences should continue to be evaluated, and the team must remember that if the replacement behavior is not reinforced, it is unlikely to be maintained after the teaching phase has been completed. If the answer is yes, then the focus should be on evaluating and improving the educational environment (e.g., instructions, routines, organization) and adjusting the contingencies.

Once the specific intervention strategy is determined, the next task is to record the specific steps of the BIP. Without such details school teams may struggle to implement the specifics of the plan, and data may not be collected with enough regularity to make meaningful data-based decisions. Umbreit et al. (2007, p. 200) advise that such a plan include several essential elements (see also Figure 9.2):

- *Behavioral definitions* of the specific target and replacement behaviors. In the example of Sarah, sitting alone would be a specific target behavior (rather than the more general "social isolation"), while initiating a conversation might be an appropriate replacement behavior.
- *Rationale or explanation* of why the target behavior was selected and how the replacement behavior will better help the student meet the educational expectations.
- *Baseline data* with a narrative description of the typical frequency, rate, duration, and/or intensity of the target and replacement behaviors prior to intervention.
- *Function of the behavior*, identifying whether the student is getting something (positive reinforcement) or avoiding or escaping something (negative reinforcement), as well as the reinforcers that appear to be involved (attention, tangibles/activities, or sensory).
- *Behavioral objective*, including a description of the conditions when the behavior is expected, the specific behavior that is expected, and the criteria for successful performance of the behavior.

Student: <u>Sarah</u>   Date: <u>Nov. 14</u>

Target behavior: Sarah sits alone at lunch and avoids contact with peers in class.

Replacement behaviors: Sitting with a peer at lunch and initiating a conversation.

Rationale: Interview and ODR data described several verbal and cyber bullying incidents involving Sarah as a target beginning in early October. Although no further bullying has been reported since those incidents were addressed, Sarah's avoidance of peers has worsened in the past month. Interview and observation data indicate that Sarah may attribute a reduction in bullying to her avoidance of all peers, resulting in negative reinforcement of her behavior.

Baseline data: Four baseline observations were made as part of the FBA, two observations occurred in class during group work, and two occurred during lunchtime. In both lunchroom observations Sarah sat alone and avoided contact with peers. During group work Sarah responded twice to peer questions ("No" and "I don't know"), and made no attempts to begin a conversation.

Intervention procedures: Two students will be recruited as peer mentors to sit with Sarah during lunch and attempt to engage her in conversation by (1) each giving her at least one compliment during lunch; and (2) each asking her an open-ended question about her interests, likes, dislikes, hobbies, and so on. These attempts will be made each day at lunch regardless of whether Sarah responds, and students will remain with Sarah until lunch is over. An in-class peer praise activity during Sarah's first-period class will also be implemented, requiring each student, including Sarah, to write a note complimenting another student in the class daily. Sarah's teacher will review these notes prior to passing them to students and will ensure that Sarah receives and gives at least one positive note each day. Conversation skills will also be taught in this class, and students will be encouraged to practice these skills during group work.

Fading and generalization: The peer praise activity will continue daily until Sarah initiates at least three conversations in a week either in class or during lunch. The activity will then be implemented weekly while observations continue. If Sarah continues to initiate at least three conversations per week, the peer praise activity will become optional. After 2 weeks of sitting with Sarah during lunch, the peer mentors will be excused from class early to ensure that they arrive in the lunchroom prior to Sarah. When Sarah arrives, they will invite her to join them. If she joins them at their table, these peers will gradually begin to invite other students to sit with this group during subsequent lunches, introducing them to Sarah. If she sits elsewhere, the intervention will be reevaluated.

Data to be collected: Four observations will be made each week, two in Sarah's first-period class and two during lunch. Observers will record conversation initiations, Sarah's responses to peers, and whether Sarah sits with peers.

Review date: December 12

Emergency procedures: If Sarah's behavior worsens, or she withdraws further when peer mentors attempt to communicate with her (e.g., moves to another table), the SWPBS team will be notified and the intervention reevaluated.

FIGURE 9.2. Sample BIP.

- *Intervention procedure*, a brief yet detailed description of the specific steps needed to carry out the selected intervention (e.g., teaching replacement behaviors, improving the environment, and/or adjusting the contingencies).
- *Fading and generalization*, a description of how the intervention will be gradually withdrawn so that the natural environment will maintain the replacement behavior, along with a plan for reinforcing or teaching the behavior in other settings (generalization) if appropriate.
- *Data to be collected*, including a description of each type of data, how frequently each type will be collected, and by whom—along with a plan for gathering treatment fidelity and social validity data (see Chapter 6). Data collected on the target and replacement behaviors should be in the same metric as the baseline data.
- *Program review date*, the time(s) at which the BIP is to be formally reviewed.
- *Personnel and role clarification*, identifying who is responsible for tasks needed to carry out the details of the BIP.
- *Emergency procedures* for unforeseen, harmful situations (increasing aggression, self-harm, etc.) that may occur during the implementation of the BIP.

Evaluation

Once the BIP is implemented, data regarding student behaviors (target and replacement) must be monitored and compared to baseline data to evaluate the effectiveness of the BIP. Changes may be necessary if data suggest that the student's behavior is not improving, if it seems to be worsening, or if the teacher or implementer finds the details of the plan not feasible. The planning team should ensure that data are collected often enough to detect behavioral changes.

Frequency of data collection will depend on the goals of the intervention. For example, if a student has typically received two office referrals per month, a monthly review of ODRs may suffice. If the student has required administrative intervention weekly, a weekly review might be necessary. Reviewing this student's ODRs only at the end of each semester would not provide timely enough information to adjust the intervention if needed. If the goal is to increase social interactions for a shy student, the number of times the student initiates a conversation may need to be recorded daily in order to meaningfully assess progress. Typically, frequent data collection is better, though the practical challenges (e.g., time, effort) associated with data collection need to be considered.

> **The planning team should ensure that data are collected often enough to detect behavioral changes.**

It is advisable when outcome data are observational in nature to measure accuracy by having a second data gatherer/observer also collect data periodically to compare with data collected by the primary observer. Although focusing on the replacement behavior should be the priority, both the target and the replacement behavior should be monitored. Many people use computer programs (e.g., Microsoft Excel) to enter and chart their BIP data, as this often eases the data monitoring task and makes changes in behavior easier to visualize (see Figure 9.3).

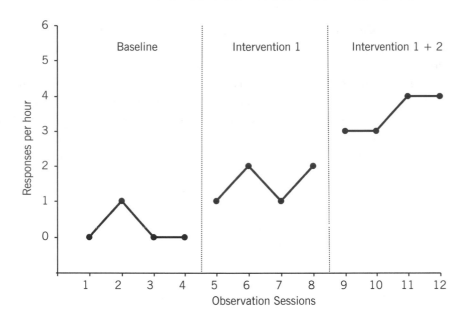

FIGURE 9.3. Sample individual behavior monitoring chart.

INDIVIDUALIZED INTERVENTIONS

Having described use of the problem-solving process in creating FBAs and BIPs, we now return to the interventions discussed in the previous chapter. When the team has gained in-depth information about the nature of a behavior problem, interventions can be tailored specifically as part of a BIP for a particular student. In the vignette at the beginning of this chapter, Cindy's repeated problematic behavior in the classroom resulted in frequent office referrals, but Cindy's behavior did not seem to be improving. Cindy's English teacher began to wonder whether the office referrals were enabling Cindy either to escape interaction with peers in the classroom or to gain more one-on-one adult attention. The planning team decided to make a careful analysis of Cindy's acting-out behavior in order to understand why existing interventions seemed to be ineffective. Creating an FBA for Cindy might begin with the question of whether avoidance of peer interaction and/or increase in attention from adults in the office contributes to Cindy's behavior. Observations and structured interviews could be designed around these questions: that is, whether Cindy was misbehaving in all settings, including those in which peer interaction or adult attention might be less involved (at the office, between classes, during lunchtime, before and after school, etc.). Thus the team could consider whether the behavior represented a "can't do" or "won't do" problem, as well as gain more information about settings that did or did not support it.

For example, if Cindy's problem behavior continued in peer settings—regardless of the absence or presence of adult attention—but became more appropriate when she was separated from peers, escape from peer interactions would appear to be its more likely function. Similarly, observations could assess the influence of adult attention on Cindy's behavior. Did Cindy misbehave in the office when adult attention was withdrawn or increased? Did her behavior improve or worsen when she was receiving individualized attention in the classroom? The answers to these questions would help tailor interventions to the student's individual needs and wants.

In Cindy's case the team learned that there were times when her behavior was appropriate in the classroom. Although frequent, her classroom misbehavior was not constant across or even within classroom settings. In fact, she did have "good days." Additionally, her behavior at the office was not always exemplary: Sometimes she refused to work even one on one, and her behavior was occasionally aggressive and inappropriate—especially when adult attention was withdrawn or the focus of interactions turned from Cindy to other work. Since these observations suggested that Cindy's behavior reflected a "won't do" rather than "can't do" situation, the team developed a behavior intervention plan with components specifically focused on Cindy's particular needs and wants. For example, Cindy's case might warrant individualized mentoring, social skills instruction, and effective contingency management.

Other interventions could be included as well, but in Cindy's situation, careful attention to these three components resolved most of her classroom behavior problems. Whereas some students might be chagrined by additional adult attention, Cindy thrived on it. In fact, her English teacher discovered that allowing Cindy to be her "assistant" and sit near her in class enabled her to withdraw attention from problematic behavior and increase attention when Cindy appropriately solicited it. This effective contingency management—reinforcement only of appropriate attention-seeking behavior—supported the individualized social skills instruction Cindy was receiving from her teacher in the classroom and school counselor outside of the classroom. As a result, Cindy's behavior greatly improved. Misbehavior in the classroom was reduced, and positive helping behaviors increased. This behavioral improvement was measured by teacher reports and a corresponding reduction in office referrals. These improvements eventually resulted in a reduced need for individualized mentoring outside the classroom.

Because Tier 3 interventions are by definition linked to the specific needs of students, there could be as many ways to individualize interventions as there are individual students requiring them. Thus rather than enumerating the many ways each intervention might be modified to meet different student needs, we use Cindy's case as an example—while individualizing the interventions to meet the needs of this student. Having effectively conducted an FBA, teams planning an intervention (BIP) should be able to similarly tailor the interventions to the needs of the students they serve.

> **Because Tier 3 interventions are by definition linked to the specific needs of students, there could be as many ways to individualize interventions as there are individual students requiring them.**

Social Skills Instruction

For Cindy, the social skills intervention could be individualized by targeting skills for appropriately eliciting teacher attention (e.g., raising her hand, asking appropriate questions, making appropriate comments, offering help). If an important function of Cindy's behavior was gaining adult attention, positive attention in response to using these skills would help Cindy learn that appropriate behavior could meet her needs better than misbehavior. Because Cindy seemed to find even negative attention reinforcing in some sense, attention (negative and positive) had to be avoided during problematic behaviors, creating a stronger contrast with positive attention for new appropriate behaviors. Such social skills may be individualized even if taught in a small group. Many opportunities for practice should be combined with positive feedback to encourage generalization of the skill.

Goal Setting

Understanding more about a student's specific behavioral deficits and excesses helps align social skills instruction not only with the student's needs and wants, but also with goal-setting aspects of intervention. For example, Cindy might be encouraged to set a goal of appropriately initiating a conversation with an adult a certain number of times per week (or to raise her hand, ask a question, offer help, etc.). Cindy's efforts to reach this goal would likely result not only in natural reinforcement from the adults she conversed with, but also attract additional attention as her teacher or mentor conducted a weekly progress review.

Social and Emotional Learning

As noted in Chapter 8, overt behavioral problems may be linked to underdeveloped social and emotional learning. Cindy was clearly seeking additional adult attention, perhaps excessively. This observation might help a team correct inappropriate attention-seeking behaviors, but behavior interventions alone may not address the underlying problems. Teaching Cindy to appropriately solicit adult attention through learning social skills and setting goals might be a step in the right direction, but these skills might not help her regulate an excessive need for adult attention. More careful analysis through appropriate assessments, interviews, or observations might have revealed that Cindy was prone to mischaracterize a lack of immediate adult attention as rejection, due in part to a misreading of emotional cues and to excessive negative self-assessment. Teaching Cindy to recognize and understand others' emotions (as well as her own), along with strategies for realistically assessing and reframing such thinking (e.g., the teacher must not like me because he or she hasn't talked to me today), might be quite effective in reducing an excessive need or desire for adult attention. Merrell's (2007a, 2007b) curriculum for social and emotional learning is an excellent resource for teaching these skills.

> **More careful analysis through appropriate assessments, interviews, or observations might have revealed that Cindy was prone to mischaracterize a lack of immediate adult attention as rejection, due in part to a misreading of emotional cues and to excessive negative self-assessment.**

Service Learning

Service learning can serve many functions, from facilitating social interactions to learning academic content. As with other interventions, a service-learning opportunity can be tailored for Tier 3 needs by aligning it with the behavioral, social, and emotional needs of the individual student as assessed in the FBA. If part of Cindy's excessive need for adult attention involved errors in thinking about her own worth or abilities, service-learning opportunities could be designed to facilitate more positive and realistic self-assessments. If Cindy could become an attention giver, rather than only an attention receiver, she might come to view herself differently. She might learn to consider giving positive attention to younger students who shared her fears and insecurities—perhaps through organizing a club or tutoring a younger student. Or Cindy might be provided opportunities to read to the elderly, serve as a student representative on a committee, or assist school staff in specific projects at the school.

Mentoring

To individualize for Cindy, a mentoring intervention could be focused on Cindy's needs and wants rather than on the needs and wants common to a group of students. Instruction in the social and emotional skills Cindy needed could be facilitated in a mentoring context with a mentor trained specifically to help Cindy move toward soliciting teacher attention in appropriate ways and contexts; learning to make more realistic self-assessments and appropriately reframe thinking errors; and gaining the ability to recognize and respond to emotional cues, and so on. When using a mentor with a student requiring intensive individualized, or multiple interventions, careful attention must be given to the maturity and capability of the mentor along with finding the best match between student and mentor. Sometimes mentors might not be appropriate at a Tier 3 level unless they receive extensive training.

Administrative Interventions

As noted in the previous chapter, students who are unresponsive to administrative interventions at a Tier 2 level may require individualized administrative support. Although the administrative intervention is by nature individualized to a certain extent, it can be distinguished at the different tiers by level of intensity and specificity. At Tier 1 all students and teachers are made aware of the process, primarily as a preventive measure. At Tier 2 students with ongoing behavior problems receive additional instruction through the administrative intervention, primarily on social skills aligned with schoolwide goals. At Tier 3 the level of intensity and specificity in an administrative intervention can be increased in several ways, which include implementing behavior contracts, tracking behavioral progress more frequently than at Tiers 1 or 2, and increasing involvement of parents or other care providers in following up with and supporting the intervention.

> At Tier 3 the level of intensity and specificity in an administrative intervention can be increased in several ways, which include implementing behavior contracts, tracking behavioral progress more frequently than at Tiers 1 or 2, and increasing involvement of parents or other care providers in following up with and supporting the intervention.

Additional opportunities for teaching and practicing appropriate behaviors with an administrator can be a thoughtful complement to other Tier 3 interventions. This additional support should be aligned with an in-depth FBA and BIP, linking administrator efforts with the problem(s) and solution(s) specified through these processes. In Cindy's case, for example, administrator teaching in response to ODRs would need to be aligned with teacher and mentor efforts to diminish inappropriate attention-seeking behaviors by teaching Cindy appropriate ways to solicit attention.

Behavioral Contracting

Behavioral contracting can be used at Tiers 1 and 2 (e.g., in helping students to reach individual or classwide goals at those levels or create group contingencies), but it is an especially useful tool for unifying supports included in a Tier 3 intervention. For example, parents can be involved in creating, signing, and following through on the contract, and checkup points for tracking progress can be included as well. At a minimum, behavior contracts should include (Black & Downs, 1993):

1. Student's name,
2. Description of the behavior(s) requiring a contract,
3. Referring teacher's name,
4. Consequences for breaking or keeping the contract,
5. Contract time frame, and
6. Signatures of student, parent, and administrator.

Contracts may also include specified replacement behaviors and rewards for successfully completing the contract. A behavior contract including these items could be a powerful motivational tool even if there is no office referral or other consequence for problematic behaviors. Teachers, mentors, counselors, and parents can use this tool as a Tier 3 component to support the teaching of replacement behaviors in conjunction with any of the interventions discussed. Additionally, these contracts can be particularly effective if school expectations and consequences (positive and negative) are aligned with expectations and consequences at home. In addition to the school consequences outlined in the following sample contract, parents might be willing to add home consequences, such as suspension of TV/Internet privileges for a time if the contract is broken or giving additional time with friends if a positive note is sent home.

One common mistake in behavioral contracting is stipulating an extended time period for good behavior. Many students will struggle to maintain a commitment in order to earn a pizza party at the end of each month. But students with challenging behaviors tend to need a combination of short- and long-term goals as well as reinforcement for reaching goals. Creating a behavior contract for a daily goal and a long-term goal tends to bring positive outcomes. For example, having a day with no tardies might earn 15 extra minutes for playing video games at home, while completing 15 days with no tardies might earn a new video game. When establishing long-term goals, some students may be less likely to give up if the required days in which successful behaviors are exhibited are not always consecutive. Going 15 consecutive days without being tardy is a worthy goal, but a student who has 14 good days may have one mishap and have to start again from the beginning, which can be very discouraging. Figure 9.4 is a behavior contract that might be arranged for Cindy.

COLLABORATING WITH COMMUNITY RESOURCES AND WRAPAROUND PROCESSES

In addition to efforts within the school and between the school and home, students with significant and chronic behavior problems often need services that are best facilitated through

Cindy's Classroom Behavior Contract
Date: October 7, 2010

This contract is being created because Cindy received an office referral from Ms. Duncan for shoving and swearing at another student in her biology class today, and because she has been sent to the office for similar incidents previously.

I, Cindy Smith, understand that if I receive another office referral for inappropriate behavior prior to the end of the term my parents will be contacted, and I will receive 1 day of in-school suspension. If I demonstrate appropriate behavior in my classes—following my teachers' instructions, and disagreeing appropriately if I have a conflict with another student—a positive note will be sent home, and I will earn up to 10 points each day for demonstrating these behaviors.

_____

Student signature

_____

Administrator signature

_____

Teacher signature

_____

Parent signature

FIGURE 9.4. Sample behavior contract.

collaboration with those providing community-based resources. Many of these students are involved in several systems: juvenile justice, child welfare, community mental health, special education, or alternative education. So a comprehensive approach to behavioral intervention will often require collaboration of an interagency team to establish reasonable goals and ensure that the students' and families' needs are consistently,

> In addition to efforts within the school and between the school and home, students with significant and chronic behavior problems often need services that are best facilitated through collaboration with those providing community-based resources.

positively, and proactively addressed. Coordination of services can be challenging because of the demands, resources, and expectations of the different systems (Eber, Sugai, Smith, & Scott, 2002).

Wraparound processes create systems of collaboration and productive relationships with support networks for students with significant behavioral and emotional problems. They focus on a community-based, integrative approach to providing services and keeping the child in the least intrusive and restrictive environment. The resulting systems of support for the youth and families may require thinking outside of the box and avoiding cookie-cutter interventions (Eber et al., 2002; Furman & Jackson, 2002). Wraparound services are not a set of predetermined interventions or services, but rather a process for planning and collaborating. Bringing together the perspectives, experiences, and expertise of a variety of professionals helps to make this process especially meaningful and effective, as youth with significant problems may tend to stretch and exhaust the family members, professionals, and systems that are working to support them (Eber et al.).

Wraparound processes make collaboration with families paramount in their function. The needs and perspectives of families guide the process of planning, which begins with identifying the strengths of the student and her or his family. The family prioritizes needs and identifies team members or other resources that they believe will be helpful to them. Eber and colleagues (2002) have carefully explained a comprehensive description of the wraparound process and its integration with a positive behavior support model.

> **Collaborating with community agencies, medical personnel, and families is essential in working with youth with severe, long-term behavioral and emotional problems.**

If a formal wraparound process is not implemented, collaborating with community agencies, medical personnel, and families is still essential in working with youth with severe, long-term behavioral and emotional problems. The following dispositions and practices can contribute to successful collaboration and outcomes (Shaw, Clayton, Dodd, & Rigby, 2004):

- Communicate successes, improvements, and effective outcomes, as well as concerns and lack of progress. Effective communication focuses on specific behavioral descriptions (e.g., Jose is sleeping in class since his medications were changed) rather than giving directives (e.g., you need to change Jose's medications).
- Recognize that professionals sometimes use different jargon. Avoiding technical language and acronyms facilitates communication. Pause to ask questions such as "What are your ideas about the intervention I just described?"
- Acknowledge operational differences. Those in different organizations may have different expectations about roles, both for themselves and for others. Different expectations may also be apparent when discussing outcomes and assumptions.
- Recognize that the number of professionals involved may concern parents—especially if they perceive mixed messages or competing solutions. If lack of progress is blamed on parents alone or on a specific agency, they may be resistant to engaging in effective collaboration. Focus on working together to find solutions.
- View parents as resources for identifying problems and understanding what resources will be most effective (Furman & Jackson, 2002). Parents know their home and youth better than any professional who is involved.
- Involve all team members. Collaboration is absolutely essential if the needs of the student and family are going to be consistently and proactively addressed. Although collaboration may be difficult when obstacles occur, trying to find solutions without collaboration between service providers will probably be more difficult.
- Focus on what can be done rather than what cannot be done. Focus on ways to work constructively within identified barriers rather than on the difficulties of doing so. Work toward consensus by asking, "What is the outcome that we all want? What can each person or agency do to facilitate that outcome?"

> **Focus on what can be done rather than what cannot be done. Focus on ways to work constructively within identified barriers rather than on the difficulties of doing so.**

- Obtain the appropriate consent/releases necessary to share information.

SUMMARY

This chapter addressed Tier 3 interventions, which differ from Tier 1 and 2 interventions in level of intensity and specificity. These interventions target individual students, specific behaviors exhibited by these students, and carefully chosen replacement behaviors and skills. Tier 3 interventions fit well within a problem-solving framework, using FBAs and BIPs. FBAs facilitate a careful examination of the ABCs of ongoing behavior problems and help planning teams better understand the nature of the problem and its functions, including the purposes behaviors might serve for students. This information helps teams to create more effective BIPs, designed to target specific behaviors and replace them with behaviors that can serve a similar function for the student in more effective and socially appropriate ways. Knowing the functions, antecedents, and consequences of behavior can also help planning teams tailor interventions already in use at Tier 2 to better meet the needs of individual students at Tier 3. Finally, Tier 3 interventions often require collaboration with service providers in the community and the formation of an interagency team. Parents play a central role in this process, helping to link services provided within the school to efforts both at home and in the wider community.

Sample FBA Interview Form

Student: _____   Date: _____

Interviewer: _____   Person being interviewed: _____

1. What is the specific behavior of concern? What does it look like when you see it? (What are the student's face, voice, hands, feet, etc., doing?)

2. What strategies have been tried to alter this behavior? What has been the result of these strategies?

3. What are some potential causes of this behavior?

4. In what setting(s) does this behavior occur? _____

5. How often does the behavior occur? _____

6. How long has this behavior been occurring? _____

7. Is there a particular time of day at which the behavior occurs? _____

8. What are the consequences when the behavior occurs?

9. What does the student find positively reinforcing?

10. What student need is being achieved with this behavior?

CHAPTER 10

Sustainability and Maintenance

When interventions and prevention efforts are designed and implemented, intentional consideration should be given for long-term sustainability of the system. If the model or strategy cannot be maintained over the long term, the feasibility and wisdom of implementing it should be critically evaluated. Sustainability should not be an afterthought or an aspect to be addressed after everything else has been done, but a crucial part of planning and ongoing implementation.

> **Sustainability should not be an afterthought or an aspect to be addressed after everything else has been done, but a crucial part of planning and ongoing implementation.**

SUSTAINABILITY

Sustainability has been defined as "The extent to which school staff or consumers can maintain the intervention over time without support from external agents" (National Association of School Psychologists, 2005, Glossary of Terms, para. 17); creating school or social norms is another meaning for the term (McIntosh, Horner, & Sugai, 2009). Sustainability can be achieved when critical factors are occurring in an effective, consistent, and efficient manner. Critical factors for sustainability, which are highly interrelated, include the following (Pool, Johnson, & Carter, 2010):

1. Strategies for maintaining teacher buy-in over time.
2. Data analysis and continued problem solving to avoid stagnation.
3. Capacity building targeted to achieve desired student outcomes.
4. Continued leadership that prioritizes implementation of SWPBS and facilitates a continuous cycle of evaluation and improvement.

All of these facets are integrally related. Continued teacher buy-in is contingent on professional development that is responsive to teacher needs, outcome data, and leadership. Outcome data will be influenced by professional development that is strategically focused on developing needed expertise. Effective leaders make professional development a priority and support teachers in making change. Successful leaders also know how to efficiently collect data and use data to make decisions. These leaders also provide recognition for progress and achievements. Having only one of these key components is insufficient: sustainability relies on all four.

FACULTY AND STAFF BUY-IN

As mentioned in Chapter 4, gaining buy-in is important before implementation begins, but faculty and staff buy-in can wane over time. Attending to buy-in is essentially measuring and responding to issues related to social validity. When the outcomes and processes of an intervention are viewed as important and reasonable, the intervention has evidence of social validity.

> **Faculty and staff will be more likely to endorse SWPBS if they are frequently shown data indicating how well outcomes are being achieved.**

Faculty and staff will be more likely to endorse SWPBS if they are frequently shown data indicating how well outcomes are being achieved. For example, presentations can be made during faculty meetings that demonstrate that ODRs are decreasing each month or that SET scores are positively changing. When faculty know that assessments of treatment integrity are related to increasing effective outcomes, they are more likely to implement interventions as planned, *and* they are more likely to observe positive changes. When teachers, parents, and students complete schoolwide surveys, time should be allotted to discuss, evaluate, and celebrate when students and parents perceive a more positive school culture than in the past. SWPBS teams should plan to consistently share outcome data with parents, teachers, and students. When outcomes are not being achieved, the problem-solving model can be used to identify barriers and challenges and then generate ideas for working through the problems.

When the authors were implementing this model in a local school, faculty meeting time was set aside to discuss data that showed the school's progress and outcomes. Often teachers would share positive experiences of change. In this school, teachers were asked to stand in the hall during passing times to provide additional supervision and to greet students by name as they entered the classroom. One teacher reported that as he intentionally focused on building a positive relationship with several students who were often quiet and withdrawn, he later noticed that these students were more likely to answer questions in class and increase participation. As positive experiences were shared, we noticed that some reluctant teachers were more likely to increase their investment in the intervention activities. When initially hesitant teachers shared their positive experiences, other teachers who had tentatively engaged in the process seemed more likely to engage with the planning team to implement the model.

Teacher buy-in and social validity measures may need to be adapted as implementation moves forward. During implementation, social validity questionnaires should consider practical considerations that are included in the survey in Form 10.1 (at the end of the chapter; based on Pool et al., 2010).

If the results of this survey or similar surveys indicate that obstacles to implementation frequently occur or that some hesitate to engage in the model, these barriers need to be addressed directly, with respect for teachers' experiences and perspectives. Focus groups can identify problems and create plans for implementing and evaluating solutions by using the problem-solving model (see Chapter 6) to work through teacher reluctance. Our experience has shown that ignoring teacher concerns or only giving them cursory attention will probably undercut efforts and outcomes.

Our experience also has shown that some teachers will probably not fully endorse SWPBS. Continued problem solving, empathic listening, and attention to their identified barriers may have little meaningful effect on their attitudes and behaviors. Reluctant teachers who are ignored have the potential to sabotage efforts, depending on the strength of their voice in the school. If the majority of teachers endorse the model and the process and the reluctant teachers are asked by the administrator to commit to the plan, these teachers seem to become "converted" to the model after the data show meaningful progress. Sometimes the loudest critics become the strongest cheerleaders over time.

DATA ANALYSIS AND CONTINUED PROBLEM SOLVING

Teams that use reliable and meaningful data can discern whether their interventions are working. Evaluating data is important in the problem-solving process; if this step is neglected, outcomes tend to be based on perceptions alone, which are usually insufficient for continued refinement and sustainability of

> **Teams that use reliable and meaningful data can discern whether their interventions are working.**

a model. Having hard data, such as ODRs, helps teachers and teams know what is working and what needs to be done next. Continuous growth and appropriate expansion of a model happens when data are evaluated to determine current needs, outcomes, and fidelity (McIntosh, Horner, et al., 2009).

If the data show that following an intervention fewer students are being referred to special education, that the number of ODRs has decreased notably over time, or that students responding to a survey feel more connected to the school (indicating a positive school climate) then team efforts will be perceived as effective and worthwhile (i.e., socially valid). Knowing that teams and individuals are achieving goals is rewarding; we tend to repeat behaviors that lead to positive results. Publicizing data that show progress often convinces naysayers that this process is valuable.

Essentially, data are considered in the context of the problem-solving model, which has been presented repeatedly through this book. Regarding sustainability, the problem-solving model can be adapted to ask these questions (McIntosh & Krugly, 2009):

1. In reviewing the data do we find that our outcomes are being achieved?
2. If not, what practices need to be modified or strengthened?
3. What is the plan for modifying our practices?
4. In reviewing the data can we conclude that modifications led to improved outcomes?

These questions help create a culture of continued evaluation and improvement. Asking these types of questions helps school teams adapt to the changing needs of students, teachers, and other stakeholders while maintaining a focus on priority outcomes.

Along with continuing to review outcome measures, understanding measures of the fidelity of intervention implementation is also vitally important. After outcomes have been achieved, implementers may become complacent because the strategies have worked so well. Teachers may assume that the interventions or prevention efforts are no longer needed; however, efforts must be continued if outcomes are to be maintained. Continuing to measure fidelity of implementation over time helps to ensure that the effectiveness of the interventions does not decrease and lead to abandoning the model (McIntosh, Horner, et al., 2009). The SET, which was first discussed in Chapter 6, is a valuable tool for assessing implementation fidelity of the core features.

> **Teams should plan to consistently share the data in a variety of settings, including faculty meetings, parent–teacher association meetings, school community council meetings, and even school board meetings.**

Sharing data with stakeholders and implementers in a timely manner will affect their investment. Teams should plan to consistently share the data in a variety of settings, including faculty meetings, parent–teacher association meetings, school community council meetings, and even school board meetings. Summaries of data could be presented via school newsletters, student newspapers, and webpages.

Evaluating the meaning of the data and using the data to solve problems and make decisions about future interventions are also critical. As discussed in Chapter 6, ODR data are usually considered a key outcome measure; other meaningful data include attendance, measures of school culture, suspensions, and academic data such as grades and test scores.

Data must be monitored over time. For example, a school team may target improving student behavior in the hallways and monitor this outcome through specifically measuring the decrease in ODRs generated in the halls. If ODRs decrease 10% each month during the first year of implementation but are not monitored in the second year, it is likely that the outcomes

> **Data analysis should consider how the data change (or do not change) over time.**

may not be sustained, and ODRs may gradually revert to preintervention levels. Outcomes should be continually monitored, even after goals have been achieved, to ensure that outcomes are maintained over time. Data analysis should consider how the data change (or do not change) over time.

Another important aspect of data analysis relevant to sustainability is to consider how students are moving through the tiers. Hopefully, students move from receiving services in Tier 3 to receiving interventions in Tier 2, and then to Tier 1. For example, if 78 students are identified and served in a Tier 2 intervention including a 6-week social skills group, and 70 of those students are eventually referred for Tier 3 interventions or special education evaluation, it could be assumed that the Tier 2 intervention had limited positive effects. This intervention may need to be more thoroughly evaluated. Maybe the needs of the students were not accurately identified through a screening process? Possibly the intervention did not match the students' needs? Or perhaps treatment integrity was inadequate?

If most students served in Tier 2 interventions are not eventually moving to Tier 1, the process needs further consideration. Similarly, if the majority of students needing and receiving individualized interventions (Tier 3) are not moving to Tier 2 interventions, several questions should be reviewed:

1. Are the interventions matching the needs of the students?
2. Are the interventions being delivered with treatment integrity?
3. Do the interventions have sufficient intensity and frequency?
4. Are the interventions intentionally targeting generalization of the new behaviors?
5. Are the new behaviors being reinforced?
6. Is there evidence of social validity of the interventions and outcomes?

Certainly some students will have chronic behavioral needs that are best addressed through continued individual supports. Ideally the goal is to teach these students new behaviors and means of self-management so that they can move away from individual supports, but realistically some students need continual high levels of support. Other students will do quite well with ongoing participation in a weekly social skills group and need few, if any, other supports.

CAPACITY DEVELOPMENT

Capacity development is creating expertise in an ongoing and systematic way (McIntosh, Horner, et al., 2009), often related to professional or teacher development. As stated in Chapter 4, teacher development concerning the SWPBS

> **Capacity development is creating expertise in an ongoing and systematic way.**

model is vital before implementation begins, but teacher development must continue over time to sustain effective implementation of efforts. Teacher development focuses on building capacity and investing in teachers and other stakeholders (McIntosh & Krugly, 2009). As capacity is built and maintained, the reliance on external experts diminishes, and reliance on internal expertise produces strong fidelity that results in effective practice and continued desired outcomes (McIntosh, Horner, et al., 2009).

Collected data can be used to determine professional development needs. For example, if decreasing ODRs has been a targeted outcome, but data do not indicate progress toward that outcome, the team should collect data related to treatment integrity of the intervention. If treatment integrity data indicate that the intervention is not being implemented as intended, highly focused professional development may be needed.

Teachers new to the school need substantial training in the model; coaching and mentoring for new teachers should include direct teaching about social skills instruction, along with pertinent information about administrative interventions, effective praise, and other key elements that have been adopted by the school. Schools need a plan to orient new teachers and staff to the SWPBS model.

Teams may choose to provide professional development only to classroom teachers during initial implementation processes; however, providing training in the model to para-educators, secretaries, custodial staff, lunchroom workers, parents, and other stakeholders will also increase sustainability efforts. Considering the specific needs of these groups will help match the training to their needs.

Finally, the focus of professional development may change as the degree of implementation increases. New challenges may emerge, student needs may change, and barriers may become apparent as the process unfolds.

> **Professional development should be responsive to change.**

Professional development should be responsive to change. Use of data from surveys and other sources should drive how and what professional development is delivered.

LEADERSHIP

> **When school administrators make sure that school teams have time to meet and plan and also arrange their own schedules to regularly attend the meetings, sustainability is more likely.**

Leadership is key in creating durable changes in schools. School administrators who actively and visibly support SWPBS over time have been central to successful implementation. When school administrators make sure that school teams have time to meet and plan and also arrange their own schedules to regularly attend the meetings, sustainability is more likely (McIntosh & Krugly, 2009). Active leadership was one of the factors that has best predicted sustainability (Doolittle, 2006).

Maintaining effective team leadership is vital to sustainability. The school-based team needs high visibility and viability in the school. Certainly some turnover in team membership is inevitable, but this should be kept to a minimum. Frequent changes in team membership are probably due to low priority of the initiative in the school or to other plans and projects that compete for insufficient resources.

Administrative priority must be observable. Faculty and staff should frequently hear the administrators emphasize that SWPBS is how business is done in the school. As the model is implemented, the climate of the school changes in a variety of positive ways that include feelings of connectedness, support, and safety (Caldarella et al., in press). Administrators can help others understand that these changes did not happen by accident, but were directly related to effective efforts, data-based decision making, and professional development.

We have consulted with schools that had administrative changes in the middle of the implementation process. For example, a new principal was hired to take the place of a highly effective principal who had made this model a very high priority. Initially, concerns were raised about the potential for sustainability with a new administrator. Fortunately, because of district and building support for the model, implementation of SWPBS was addressed when candidates were interviewed and selected. The new principal was excited about the changes happening in the school and showed enthusiasm to continue the work. However, she did not initially have the information and background needed to continue the very visible leadership provided by the outgoing principal. With the support of her school-based team, district leaders, and individual study, she was soon fully competent with the strategies being used and provided meaningful insights about the data.

> **Processes and procedures that are codified in written policy are more likely to withstand the test of time.**

Processes and procedures that are codified in written policy are more likely to withstand the test of time. Policies reflect the ingrained culture of the school, and changes in the culture due to SWPBS should be noted in mission statements, school improvement plans, and so on. As building and team leaders intentionally change school policies to reflect SWPBS practices, sustainability is supported (McIntosh & Krugly, 2009).

One of the most challenging aspects of leadership is managing new priorities, programs, and mandates. Change that focuses on continual improvement is vital to developing and sustaining quality educational programs, and managing that change is a challenge. Faculty and staff of schools with a history of repeatedly implementing new programs and abandoning them tend to be less invested in change and may be cynical about sustainability. Effective leaders manage this change process by identifying priorities and evaluating ways new ideas will contribute or distract from achieving desired outcomes. They maintain the course of change while efficiently adapting to evolving needs. Describing the effects of abandoning practices may help when competing programs are proposed (McIntosh & Krugly, 2009). Successful leaders respect the resources in their buildings, and they are careful not to implement change unless needed resources are available and can be maintained.

Finally, leaders acknowledge successes, efforts, and progress. They create times to openly celebrate and share data with stakeholders, especially those with resources to contribute to future efforts. They acknowledge and reinforce achievements, perhaps by providing lunches to celebrate positive outcomes or giving gift certificates for teachers who have written a predetermined number of praise notes. Celebrating successes on bulletin boards in highly visible areas is another way to acknowledge progress; parents can be encouraged to review a bulletin board at back-to-school night or parent–teacher conferences. Newsletters and websites are additional forums for sharing group and individual success stories. Acknowledging individuals and groups that achieve outcomes and make consistent effort contributes to the support for and thus sustainability of this model.

SUMMARY

Developing and implementing a continuum of services for youth with behavioral and emotional concerns requires time, focus, teamwork, and reflection. When implemented with fidelity and focus, these efforts can result in meaningful positive outcomes for youth and organizations. School teams that simultaneously focus on academic achievement and social–emotional well-being for *all* students will be able to actively and effectively address student needs.

Survey to Assess Social Validity during Implementation of SWPBS

	Strongly disagree	Disagree	Neither agree or disagree	Agree	Strongly agree
I have the materials I need to implement SWPBS.					
I have the knowledge I need to implement SWPBS.					
The expectations for me to implement SWPBS are clearly communicated.					
The school team responsible for SWPBS communicates information in a timely manner.					
District and school policies support SWPBS.					
I am eager to implement SWPBS strategies.					
We are collecting data that will help us determine meaningful outcomes.					
I know what our school data for SWPBS communicates about our efforts.					
I have seen improvements in school culture since implementing SWPBS.					
I believe my efforts are important contributions to our outcomes.					
What is going well with SWPBS implementation?					
What needs to be improved with SWPBS implementation?					

References

Alfonso, V. C., Rentz, E., Orlovsky, K., & Ramos, E. (2007). Test review: School Social Behavior Scales, Second Edition. *Journal of Psychoeducational Assessment, 25*(1), 82–92.

Anderman, E. M. (2002). School effects on psychological outcomes during adolescence. *Journal of Educational Psychology, 94*(4), 795–809.

Batsche, G. (n.d.). *Building support.* Retrieved June 8, 2010, from *www.rtinetwork.org/Get-Started/BuildSupport/ar/BuildingSupport.*

Birman, D., & Chan, W. Y. (2008). *Screening and assessing immigrant and refugee youth in school-based mental health programs.* Retrieved June 8, 2010, from *www.rwjf.org/files/research/3320.32211.0508issuebriefno.1.pdf.*

Black, D. D., & Downs, J. C. (1987). *The administrative intervention workshop manual.* Omaha, NE: Father Flanagan's Boys Town.

Black, D. D., & Downs, J. C. (1993). *Administrative intervenion: A school administrator's guide to working with aggressive and disruptive students* (2nd ed.). Longmont, CO: Sopris West.

Bouchey, H. A., & Harter, S. (2005). Reflected appraisals, academic self-perceptions, and math/science performance during early adolescence. *Journal of Educational Psychology, 97,* 673–686.

Bradshaw, C. P., Reinke, W. M., Brown, L. D., & Leaf, P. L. (2008). Implementation of schoolwide positive behavior interventions and supports (PBIS) in elementary schools: Observations from a randomized trial. *Education and Treatment of Children, 31*(1), 1–26.

Brand, S., Felner, R., Seitsinger, A., Burns, A., & Bolton, N. (2008). A large scale study of the assessment of the social environment of middle and secondary schools: The validity and utility of teachers' ratings of school climate, cultural pluralism, and safety problems for understanding school effects and school improvement. *Journal of School Psychology, 46*(5), 507–535.

Brookmeyer, K. A., Fanti, K. A., & Henrich, C. C. (2006). Schools, parents, and youth violence: A multilevel, ecological analysis. *Journal of Clinical & Child Adolescent Psychology, 35*(4), 504–514.

Burnett, P. C. (2002). Teacher praise and feedback and students' perceptions of the classroom environment. *Educational Psychology, 22*(1), 5–16.

Burns, M. K., & Gibbons, K. (2008). *Implementing response-to-intervention in elementary and secondary schools: Procedures to assure scientific-based practices.* New York: Routledge.

Caldarella, P., Adams, M. B., Valentine, S., & Young, K. R. (2009). Evaluation of a mentoring program for elementary school students at risk for emotional and behavioral disorders. *New Horizons in Education, 57*(1), 1–16.

Caldarella, P., & Merrell, K. (1997). Common dimensions of social skills of children and adolescents: A taxonomy of positive behaviors. *School Psychology Review, 26,* 264–278.

Caldarella, P., Shatzer, R. H., Gray, K. M., Young, K. R., & Young, E. L. (in press). The effects of schoolwide positive behavior support on middle school climate and student outcomes. *Research in Middle Level Education Online.*

Caldarella, P., Young, E. L., Richardson, M. J.,

Young, B. J., & Young, K. R. (2008). Validation of the systematic screening for behavior disorders in middle and junior high school. *Journal of Emotional and Behavioral Disorders, 16*(2), 105–117.

California Department of Education. (2009). *California Healthy Kids Survey.* Retrieved June 8, 2010, from *www.wested.org/cs/chks/view/chks_s/2?x-layout=surveys.*

Chapin, J., & Gleason, D. (2004). Student perceptions of school violence: Could it happen here? *Journal of Adolescent Research, 19*(3), 360–376.

Chartier, M., Vander Stoep, A., McCauley, E., Herting, J. R., Tracy, M., & Lymp, J. (2008). Passive versus active parental permission: Implications for the ability of school-based depression screening to reach youth at risk. *Journal of School Health, 78*(3), 157–164.

Clonan, S. M., McDougal, J. L., Clark, K., & Davison, S. (2007). Use of office discipline referrals in school-wide decision making: A practical example. *Psychology in the Schools, 44*(1), 19.

Cohen, J. (2007, fall). *Evaluating and improving school climate: Creating a climate for learning.* Retrieved June 8, 2010, from *www.nais.org/publications/ismagazinearticle.cfm?ItemNumber=150284.*

Collins, W. A., & Laursen, B. (2004a). Changing relationships, changing youth: Interpersonal contexts of adolescent development. *Journal of Early Adolescence, 24,* 55–62.

Collins, W. A., & Laursen, B. (2004b). Parent–adolescent relationships and influences. In R. Lerner & L. Steinberg (Eds.), *Handbook of adolescent psychology* (pp. 331–361). New York: Wiley.

Crone, D. A., & Horner, R. H. (2003). *Building positive behavior support systems in schools: Functional behavioral assessment.* New York: Guilford Press.

Dahl, R. E., & Hariri, A. R. (2005). Lessons from G. Stanley Hall: Connecting new research in biological sciences to the study of adolescent development. *Journal of Research on Adolescence, 15,* 367–382.

Dappen, L. D., & Isernhagen, J. C. (2005). Developing a student mentoring program: Building connections for at-risk students. *Preventing School Failure, 49*(3), 21–25.

Darling-Hammond, L., Wei, R. C., Andree, A., Richardson, N., & Orphanos, S. (2009). *Professional learning in the learning profession: A status report on teacher development in the United States and abroad.* Dallas: National Staff Development Council.

Deal, T. E., & Peterson, K. D. (1999). *Shaping school culture: The heart of leadership.* San Francisco: Jossey-Bass.

Deal, T. E., & Peterson, K. D. (2009). *Shaping school culture: Pitfalls, paradoxes, and promises* (2nd ed). San Francisco: Jossey-Bass.

Doolittle, J. H. (2006). *Sustainability of positive behavior supports in schools.* Unpublished doctoral dissertation, University of Oregon, Eugene, OR.

Drummond, T. (1994). *The Student Risk Screening Scale (SRSS).* Grants Pass, OR: Josephine County Mental Health Program.

Eber, L., Sugai, G., Smith, C., & Scott, T. (2002). Wraparound and positive behavioral interventions and supports in the schools. *Journal of Emotional and Behavioral Disorders, 10*(3), 171.

Eccles, J. S. (2004). Schools, academic motivation, and stage-environment fit. In R. Lerner & L. Steinberg (Eds.), *Handbook of adolescent psychology* (pp. 125–153). New York: Wiley.

Eccles, J. S., Lord, S., & Midgely, C. (1991). What are we doing to early adolescents? The impact of educational contexts on early adolescents. *American Journal of Education, 99*(4), 521–542.

Eccles, J. S., Midgley, C., Wigfield, A., Buchanan, C. M., Reuman, D., Flanagan, C., et al. (1993). Development during adolescence: The impact of stage–environment fit on young adolescents' experiences in schools and in families. *American Psychologist, 48,* 90–101.

Evans, T. (1997). The tools of encouragement. *Reaching Today's Youth, 1*(2), 10–14.

Fenning, P. (2004). Engaging staff and students to implement positive behavior support in their high school. In H. Bohanon-Edmonson, K. B. Flannery, L. Eber, & B. Sugai (Eds.), *Positive behavioral support in high schools: Monograph from the 2004 Illinois High School Forum of Positive Behavioral Interventions and Supports* (pp. 35–44). Retrieved June 8, 2010, from *www.pbis.org.*

Finn, C. A., & Sladeczek, I. E. (2001). Assessing the social validity of behavioral interventions: A review of treatment acceptability measures. *School Psychology Quarterly, 16*(2), 176–206.

Flannery, B. K., Sugai, G., & Anderson C. M. (2009). School-wide positive behavior support in high school: Early lessons learned. *Journal of Positive Behavior Interventions, 11*(3), 177–185.

Florida Department of Education. (2006). *Collaborative problem solving.* Retrieved June 8, 2010, from *sss.usf.edu/504tutorial/Module2/CollabProbSolving.html.*

Freiberg, H. J. (1999). *School climate: Measuring, improving and sustaining healthy learning environments.* Philadelphia: Falmer Press.

Furman, R., & Jackson, R. (2002). Wrap-around services: An analysis of community-based mental health services for children. *Journal of Child and Adolescent Psychiatric Nursing, 15*(3), 124.

Garet, M. S., Porter, A. C., Desimone, L., Birman, B. F., & Yoon, K. S. (2001). What makes professional development effective? Results from a national sample of teachers. *American Educational Research Journal, 38*(4), 915–945.

Garrison, W. M. (2004). Profiles of classroom practices in U.S. public schools. *School Effectiveness and School Improvement, 15*(3), 377–406.

George, H. P., Harrower, J. K., & Knoster, T. (2003). School-wide prevention and early intervention: A process for establishing a system of school-wide behavior support. *Preventing School Failure, 47*(4), 170–176.

Glover, T. A., & Albers, C. A. (2007). Considerations for evaluating universal screening assessments. *Journal of School Psychology, 45*, 117–135.

Goldstein, A. P. (1999). *The prepare curriculum: Teaching prosocial competencies.* Champaign, IL: Research Press.

Goldstein, A. P., & McGinnis, E. (1997). *Skillstreaming the adolescent: New strategies and perspectives for teaching social skills.* Champaign, IL: Research Press.

Goldstein, A. P., McGinnis, E., Sprafkin, R. P., Gershaw, J., & Klein, P. (1997). *Skillstreaming the adolescent: Student manual.* Champaign, IL: Research Press.

Grayson, J. L., & Alvarez, H. K. (2008). School climate factors relating to teacher burnout: A mediator model. *Teaching and Teacher Education, 24*(5), 1349–1363.

Halawah, I. (2005). The relationship between effective communication of high school principal and school climate. *Education, 126*(2), 334–345.

Hansen, J., & Childs, J. (1998). Creating a school where people like to be. *Educational Leadership, 56*(1), 14.

Harter, S., & Monsour, A. (1992). Developmental analysis of conflict caused by opposing attributes in the adolescent self-portrait. *Developmental Psychology, 28*, 251–260.

Haynes, N. M., Emmons, C., & Ben-Avie, M. (1997). School climate as a factoring student adjustment and achievement. *Journal of Educational and Psychological Consultation, 8*, 321–329.

Heck, R. H. (2000). Examining the impact of school quality on school outcomes and improvement: A value added approach. *Educational Administration Quarterly, 36*(4), 513–552.

Herman, K. C., Merrell, K. W., Reinke, W. M., & Tucker, C. M. (2004). The role of school psychology in preventing depression. *Psychology in the Schools, 41*, 763–775.

Hinckley, G. B. (2000). *Standing for something: 10 neglected virtues that will heal our hearts and homes.* New York: Times Books.

Holcomb, E. L. (2004). *Getting excited about data* (2nd ed.). Thousand Oaks, CA: Corwin Press.

Holcomb-McCoy, C. (2005). Ethnic identity development in early adolescence: Implications and recommendations for middle school counselors. *Professional School Counseling, 9*, 120–127.

Horner, R. H., Sugai, G., & Todd, A. W. (2001). Data need not be a four-letter word: Using data to improve schoolwide discipline. *Beyond Behavior, 11*(1), 20–26.

Hoy, W. K., & Hannum, J. W. (1997). Middle school climate: An empirical assessment of organizational health and student achievement. *Educational Administration Quarterly, 33*(3), 290–311.

Jacob, S., & Hartshorne, T. S. (2007). *Ethics and the law for school psychologists* (5th ed.). Hoboken, NJ: Wiley.

Jacobson, S. E. (2009). *Students' perceptions and experiences of secondary public school safety.* Unpublished manuscript, Counseling Psychology and Special Education Department, Brigham Young University, Provo, UT.

Jennings, D. (n.d.). *Debra Jennings: Engaging families in RTI.* Retrieved June 8, 2010, from *www.rtinetwork.org/professional/podcasts/debra-jennings-engaging-families-in-rti.*

Kamphaus, R. W., & Reynolds, C. R. (2007). *BASC-2 Behavioral and Emotional Screening System,* Minneapolis: Pearson.

Kaplan, L. S., & Owings, W. A. (2002). Enhancing teaching quality. *Phi Delta Kappa Fastbacks, 499*, 3–44.

Keating, D. P. (2004). Cognitive and brain development. In R. Lerner & L. Steinberg (Eds.), *Handbook of adolescent psychology* (pp. 45–84). New York: Wiley.

Kelley, R. C., Thornton, B., & Daugherty, R. (2005). Relationships between measures of leadership and school climate. *Education, 126*(1), 17–25.

Kern, L., Dunlap, G., Clarke, S., & Childs, K. E. (1994). Student-assisted functional assessment interview. *Diagnostique, 19,* 20–39.

Kerr, M. M., & Nelson, C. M. (2006). *Strategies for addressing behavior problems in the classroom* (5th cd.). Upper Saddle River, NJ: Prentice Hall.

Kitsantas, A., Ware, H. W., & Martinez-Arias, R. (2004). Students' perceptions of school safety: Effects of community, school environment, and substance use variables. *Journal of Early Adolescence, 24*(4), 412–430.

Lane, K. L., & Beebe-Frankenberger, M. (2004). *School-based interventions: The tools you need to succeed.* Boston: Pearson Education.

Lane, K. L., Carter, E. W., Pierson, M. R., & Glaeser, B. C. (2006). Academic, social, and behavioral characteristics of high school students with emotional disturbances or learning disabilities. *Journal of Emotional and Behavioral Disorders, 14*(2), 108–117.

Lane, K. L., Kalber, J. R., Bruhn, A. L., Driscoll, S. A., Wehby, J. H., & Elliott, S. N. (2009). Assessing social validity of school-wide positive behavior support plans: Evidence for the reliability and structure for the primary intervention rating scale. *School Psychology Review, 38*(1), 135–144.

Lane, K. L., Kalberg, J. R., Parks, R. J., & Carter, E. W. (2008). Student Risk Screening Scale: Initial evidence for score reliability and validity at the high school level. *Journal of Emotional and Behavioral Disorders, 16*(3), 178–190.

Lane, K. L., Parks, R. J., Kalberg, J. R., & Carter, E. W. (2007). Systematic screening at the middle school level: Score reliability and validity of the Student Risk Screening Scale. *Journal of Emotional and Behavioral Disorders, 15*(4), 209–222.

Lane, K. L., Wehby, J., & Barton-Arwood, S. M. (2005). Students with and at risk for emotional and behavioral disorders: Meeting their social and academic needs. *Preventing Social Failure, 49*(2), 6–9.

Leithwood, K., Mascall, B., Strauss, T., Sacks, R., Memon, N., & Yashkina, A. (2007). Distributing leadership to make schools smarter: Taking the ego out of the system. *Leadership and Policy in Schools, 6*(1), 37–67.

Levitt, J. M., Saka, N., Romanelli, L. H., & Hoagwood, K. (2007). Early identification of mental health problems in schools: The status of instrumentation. *Journal of School Psychology, 45,* 163–191.

Lindsey, B. C., & White, M. (2010). Tier 1 case example: School-wide information system (SWIS). In J. P. Clark & M. Alvarez (Eds.), *Response to intervention: A guide for school social workers* (pp. 55–69). New York: Oxford University Press.

Little, E. (2005). Secondary school teachers' perception of students' problem behaviours. *Educational Psychology, 25,* 369–377.

Marchant, M., Anderson, D. H., Caldarella, P., Fisher, A., Young, B. J., & Young, K. R. (2009). Schoolwide screening and programs of positive behavior support: Informing the intervention process. *Preventing School Failure, 53*(3), 131–143.

Marchant, M., Brown, M., Caldarella, P., & Young, E. (2010). Effects of Strong Kids curriculum on students at risk for internalizing disorders: A pilot study. *Journal of Empirically Based Practices in Schools, 11*(2), 123–143.

Marchant, M., & Young, K. R. (2001). The effects of a parent coach on parents' acquisition and implementation of parenting skills. *Education and Treatment of Children, 24,* 351–373.

Marcia, J. E. (2002). Adolescence, identity and the Bernardone family. *Identity: An International Journal of Theory and Research, 2,* 199–209.

Mass-Galloway, R. L., Panyan, M. V., Smith, C. R., & Wessendorf, S. (2008). Systems change with school-wide positive behavior supports. *Journal of Positive Behavior Interventions, 10*(2), 129.

McGuire, J. K., & Gamble, W. C. (2006). Community service for youth: The value of psychological engagement over number of hours spent. *Journal of Adolescence, 29,* 289–298.

McIntosh, K., Horner, R. H., & Sugai, G. (2009). Sustainability of systems-level evidenced-based practices in schools: Current knowledge and future directions. In W. Sailor, G. Sugai, R. H. Horner, & G. Dunlap (Eds.), *Handbook of positive behavior support* (pp. 327–352). New York: Springer.

McIntosh, K. & Krugly, A. (2009). Sustaining school-wide PBS: The principal's perspective. Retrieved June 8, 2010, from *www.pbis.org/ common/cms/documents/Forum_09_Presenta- tions/Sustainability_D1.pdf*.

McIntosh, K., Reinke, W. M., & Herman, K. C. (2009). Schoolwide analysis of data for social behavior problems: Assessing outcomes, select- ing targets for intervention, and identifying need for support. In G. Peacock, R. Ervin, E. Daly, & K. Merrell (Eds.), *Practical handbook of school psychology: Effective practices for the 21st century* (pp. 135–156). New York: Guilford Press.

Merrell, K. W. (2007a). *Strong kids, grades 6–8: A social and emotional learning curriculum*. Bal- timore: Brookes.

Merrell, K. W. (2007b). *Strong teens, grades 9–12: A social and emotional learning curriculum*. Baltimore: Brookes.

Merrell, K. W. (2008). *School Social Behavior Scales, Second Edition*. Baltimore: Brookes.

Merrell, K. W., & Gimpel, G. A. (1998). *Social skills of children and adolescents: Conceptu- alization, assessment, treatment*. Mahwah, NJ: Erlbaum.

Merrell, K. W., & Gueldner, B. A. (2010). *Social and emotional learning in the classroom: Pro- moting mental health and academic success*. New York: Guilford Press.

Metzler, C. W., Biglan, A., Rusby, J. C., & Sprague, J. R. (2001). Evaluation of a comprehensive be- havior management program to improve school- wide positive behavior support. *Education and Treatment of Children, 24*(4), 448–479.

Mihalic, S. (2004). The importance of implemen- tation fidelity. *Emotional and Behavioral Dis- orders in Youth, 4*(4), 83–105.

Morgan-D'Atrio, C., Northup, J., LaFleur, L., & Spera, S. (1996). Toward prescriptive alterna- tives to suspensions: A preliminary evaluation. *Behavioral Disorders, 21*, 190–200.

Moroz, K. B., & Jones, K. M. (2002). The effects of positive peer reporting on children's social involvement. *School Psychology Review, 31*(2), 235–245.

Muijs, D., Harris, A., Chapman, C., Stoll, L., & Russ, J. (2004). Improving schools in socioeco- nomically disadvantaged areas—A review of research evidence. *School Effectiveness and School Improvement, 15*(2), 149–175.

Murphy, J. A., & Pimentel, S. (1996). Grading principals: Administrator evaluations come of age. *Phi Delta Kappan, 78*(1), 74–81.

Myles, B., Moran, M. R., Ormsbee, C. K., & Down- ing, J. A. (1992). Guidelines for establishing and maintaining token economies. *Intervention in School and Clinic, 27*(3), 164–169.

National Association of School Psychologists. (2005). *Position statement on prevention and intervention research in the schools*. Retrieved June 8, 2010, from *www.nasponline.org/about_ nasp/pp_prevresearch.aspx*.

National Research Council. (2004). *Engaging schools: Fostering high school students' moti- vation to learn*. Washington, DC: National Aca- demic Press.

National Research Council and Institute of Medi- cine. (2009). *Preventing mental, emotional, and behavioral disorders among young people: Progress and possibilities*. Washington, DC: National Academies Press.

Nelson, J. A. P., Caldarella, P., Young, K. R., & Webb, N. (2008). Using peer praise notes to increase the social involvement of withdrawn adolescents. *Teaching Exceptional Children, 41*, 6–13.

Nelson, J. A. P., Young, B. J., Young, E. L., & Cox, G. (2010). Utilizing teacher-written praise notes to promote a positive environment in a middle school. *Preventing School Failure, 54*(2), 119– 125.

Nelson, J. R., Gonzales, J. E., Epstein, M. H., & Benner, G. J. (2003). Administrative discipline contacts: A review of the literature. *Behavioral Disorders, 28*, 249–281.

Niesyn, M. E. (2009). Strategies for success: Evidence-based instructional practices for students with emotional and behavioral dis- orders. *Preventing School Failure, 53*(4), 227– 234.

Office of Special Education Programs. (n.d.). *School-wide positive behavior support: Im- plementers' blueprint and self-assessment*. Retrieved June 8, 2010, from *www.osepide- asthatwork.org/toolkit/pdf/SchoolwideBehav- iorSupport.pdf*.

Olsson, C. A., Bond, L., Burns, J. M., Vella- Brodrick, D. A., & Sawyer, S. M. (2003). Ado- lescent resilience: A concept analysis. *Journal of Adolescence, 26*, 1–11.

O'Neill, R. E., Horner, R. H., Albin, R. W., Storey, K., & Sprague, J. R. (1997). *Functional analy- sis of problem behavior: A practical assessment guide* (2nd ed.). Pacific Grove, CA: Brookes/Cole.

Parent Engagement in Colorado School-Wide PBS Schools. (n.d.). Retrieved June 8, 2010, from *www.pbis.org/common/cms/documents/Parent/IdeasToEngageParents/35waystoengageparentscoloradoexample.pdf*.

Peterson, L., Young, K. R., Salzberg, C. S., & West, R. R. (2006). Using self-management procedures to improve classroom social skills in multiple general education settings. *Education and Treatment of Children, 29*(1), 1–21.

Phinney, J. S. (1989). Stages of ethnic identity development in minority group adolescents. *Journal of Early Adolescence, 9*, 34–49.

Plucker, J. A. (1998). The relationship between school climate conditions and student aspirations. *Journal of Educational Research, 91*(4), 240–246.

Pool, J. L., Johnson, E. S., & Carter, D. R. (2010). *Implementing a combined RTI/PBS model: Social validity.* Retrieved June 8, 2010, from *www.rtinetwork.org/rti-blog/entry/1/97*.

Protection of Pupil Rights Amendment. (n.d.). Retrieved June 8, 2010, from *www2.ed.gov/policy/gen/guid/fpco/ppra/index.html*.

Reddy, L. A., Newman, E., De Thomas, C. A., & Chun, V. (2009). Effectiveness of school-based prevention and intervention programs for children and adolescents with emotional disturbance: A meta-analysis. *Journal of School Psychology, 47*, 77–99.

Renshaw, T., Young, K. R., Caldarella, P., & Christensen, L. (2008). *Can school-wide positive behavior support be an evidence-based practice?* Provo, UT: Brigham Young University. (ERIC Document Reproduction Service No. ED506271)

Reynolds, C. W., & Kamphaus, R. W. (2004). *Behavioral Assessment System for Children, Second Edition.* Minneapolis: Pearson.

Richardson, M. J., Caldarella, P., Young, B. J., Young, E. L., & Young, K. R. (2009). Further validation of the Systematic Screening for Behavior Disorders in middle and junior high school. *Psychology in the Schools, 46*(7), 605–615.

Richardson, M. J., Sabbah, H. Y., Juchau, A. T., Caldarella, P., & Young, E. L. (2007). *Exploring perceptions of school quality: Implications for school administrators.* Provo, UT: Brigham Young University Positive Behavior Support Initiative. (ERIC Document Reproduction Service No. ED501833)

Ringeisen, H., Henderson, K., & Hoagwood, K. (2003). Context matters: Schools and the "research to practice gap" in children's mental health. *School Psychology Review, 22*, 153–168.

Ruus, V., Veisson, M., Leino, M., Ots, L., Pallas, L., Sarv, E., et al. (2007). Students' well-being, coping, academic success, and school climate. *Social Behavior and Personality, 35*(7), 919–936.

Sadler, C. (2000). Effective behavior support implementation at the district level: Tigard-Tualatin School District. *Journal of Positive Behavior Interventions, 2*, 241–243.

Sailor, W., Bradley, R., & Sims, B. (2009, October). *Integrating data systems for RTI implementation.* Paper presented at the National Positive Behavioral Interventions and Support Forum, Rosemont, IL.

Samdal, O., Wold, B., & Bronis, M. (1999). Relationship between students' perceptions of school environment, their satisfaction with school and perceived academic achievement: An international study. *School Effectiveness and School Improvement, 10*(3), 296–320.

Sandomierski, T., Kincaid, D., & Algozzine, B. (2007). Response to intervention and positive behavior support: Brothers from different mothers or sisters with different misters? *PBIS Newsletter, 4*(2). Retrieved June 8, 2010, from *www.pbis.org/pbis_newsletter/volume_4/issue2.aspx*.

Severson, H. H., Walker, H. M., Hope-Doolittle, J., Kratochwill, T. R., & Gresham, F. M. (2007). Proactive, early screening to detect behaviorally at-risk students: Issues, approaches, emerging innovations, and professional practices. *Journal of School Psychology, 45*, 193–223.

Shaw, S. R., Clayton, M. C., Dodd, J. L., & Rigby, B. T. (2004). *Collaborating with physicians: A guide for school leaders.* Retrieved June 8, 2010, from *www.nasponline.org/resources/principals/nassp_collab.aspx*.

Sidman, M. (1989). *Coercion and its fallout.* Boston: Authors Cooperative.

Smetana, J. G., & Bitz, B. (1996). Adolescents' conceptions of teachers' authority and their relations to rule violations in school. *Child Development, 67*, 1153–1172.

Society for Adolescent Medicine. (2003). Corporal punishment in schools: Position paper of the

Society for Adolescent Medicine. *Journal of Adolescent Health, 32,* 385–393.

Sprague, J. R., Sugai, G., Horner, R., & Walker, H. M. (1999). Using office discipline referral data to evaluate school-wide discipline and violence prevention interventions. *Oregon School Study Council, 42*(2), 1–18.

Steinberg, L. D. (2008). *Adolescence* (8th ed.). Boston: McGraw-Hill.

Sterbinsky, A., Ross, S., & Redfield, D. (2006). Effects of comprehensive school reform on student achievement and school change: A longitudinal multi-site study. *School Effectiveness and School Improvement, 17*(3), 367–397.

Stott, K. A., & Jackson, A. P. (2005). Using service-learning to achieve middle school comprehensive guidance program goals. *Professional School Counseling, 9*(2), 156–159.

Sugai, G. (2002). *School-wide discipline and PBS,* Colorado Department of Education. Retrieved June 8, 2010, from *www.cde.state.co.us/pbs/Presentations04.asp.*

Sugai, G., & Horner, R. H. (2006). A promising approach for expanding and sustaining school-wide positive behavior support. *School Psychology Review, 35,* 245–259.

Sugai, G., Horner, R. H., Algozzine, R., Barrett, S., Lewis, T., Anderson, C., et al. (2010). *School-wide positive behavior support: Implementers' blueprint and self-assessment.* Eugene: University of Oregon. Retrieved June 8, 2010, from *www.pbis.org/common/pbisresources/publications/SWPBS_Implementation_Blueprint_v_May_9_2010.pdf.*

Sugai, G., Lewis-Palmer, T., Todd, A., & Horner, R. H. (2001). *School-wide evaluation tool.* Eugene: University of Oregon.

Susman, E. J., & Rogol, A. (2004). Puberty and psychological development. In R. Lerner & L. Steinberg (Eds.), *Handbook of adolescent psychology* (pp. 15–44). New York: Wiley.

Sutherland, K., Wehby, J., & Copeland, S. (2000). Effect of varying rates of behavior-specific praise on the on-task behavior of students with EBD. *Journal of Emotional and Behavioral Disorders, 8,* 2–8.

Taylor, M., West, R., & Smith, T. (2006). *The Indicators of School Quality (ISQ) Survey manual.* Logan, UT: Center for the School of the Future.

Taylor-Greene, S., Brown, D., Nelson, L., Longton, J., Gassman, T., Cohen, J., et al. (1997).

School-wide behavioral support: Starting the year off right. *Journal of Behavioral Education, 7*(1), 99–112.

Tobin, T. J., Lewis-Palmer, T., & Sugai, G. (2002). School-wide and individualized effective behavior: An explanation and an example. *Behavior Analysis Today, 3*(1), 51–75.

Tobin, T. J., Sugai, G., & Colvin, G. (2000). Using discipline referrals to make decisions. *NASSP Bulletin, 84*(616), 106–117.

Townsend, T. (1997). What makes schools effective? A comparison between school communities in Australia and the USA. *School Effectiveness and School Improvement, 8*(3), 311–326.

Turnbull, A., Edmonson, H., Griggs, P., Wickham, D., Sailor, W., Freeman, R., et al. (2002). A blueprint for school-wide positive behavior support: Implementation of three components. *Exceptional Children, 68,* 377–402.

Umbreit, J., Ferro, J. B., Liaupsin, C. J., & Lane, K. L. (2007). *Functional behavioral assessment and function-based intervention: An effective, practical approach.* Upper Saddle River, NJ: Pearson Education.

Wagner, M., Kutash, K., Duchnowski, A. J., Epstein, M. H., & Sumi, W. C. (2005). The children and youth we serve: A national picture of the characteristics of students with emotional disturbances receiving special education. *Journal of Emotional and Behavioral Disorders, 13*(2), 79–96.

Walker, H. M., Ramsey, E., & Gresham, F. (2004). *Antisocial behavior in school* (2nd ed.). Belmont, CA: Wadsworth Thomson Learning.

Walker, H. M., & Severson, H. H. (1992). *Systematic Screening for Behavior Disorders (SSBD).* Longmont, CO: Sopris West.

West, R. P., Young, K. R., Callahan, K., Fister, S., Kemp, K., Freston, J., et al. (1995). Managing the classroom behavior of secondary-aged students: The musical clocklight. *Teaching Exceptional Children, 27,* 46–51.

Witziers, B., Bosker, R. J., & Kruger, M. L. (2003). Educational leadership and student achievement: The elusive search for an association. *Educational Administration Quarterly, 39*(3), 398.

Wright, J., & Dusek, J. (1998). Compiling school base-rates for disruptive behavior from student disciplinary referral data. *School Psychology Review, 27*(1), 138.

Yates, M., & Youniss J. (1996). Community service and political-moral identity in adolescents. *Journal of Research on Adolescence, 6*(3), 271–284.

Young, E. L., Sabbah, H., Young, B. J., Reiser, M., & Richardson, M. (2010). Gender differences and similarities in a screening process for emotional and behavioral risk in secondary schools. *Journal of Emotional and Behavioral Disorders, 18*, 225–235.

Young, K. R., West, R. P., Marchant, M., Mitchem, K., Christensen, L., Young, J. R., et al. (2008). *Building positive relationships and social skills: A nurturing pedagogy approach.* Provo, UT: Brigham Young University Positive Behavior Support Initiative.

Young, K. R., West, R. P., Smith, D. J., & Morgan, D. P. (1991). *Teaching self-management strategies to adolescents.* Longmont, CO: Sopris West.

Zins, J. E., Bloodworth, M. R., Weissberg, R. P., & Walberg, H. J. (2007). The scientific base linking social and emotional learning to school success. *Journal of Educational and Psychological Consultation, 17*(2/3), 191–210.

Index